The Man in the Straw Hat

The Man in the Straw Hat

MY STORY

by Maurice Chevalier

THOMAS Y. CROWELL COMPANY • NEW YORK

Translated by Caroline Clark

Designed by Maurice Serle Kaplan

Manufactured in the United States of America by the Cornwall Press, Inc., Cornwall, New York

---

ACKNOWLEDGMENT is made to Maurice Chevalier; The Albert Davis Collection; Paramount Pictures, Inc.; Pix, Inc.; and Wide World Photos for permission to reproduce photographs in this book.

Contents

Contents

Illustrations

Illustrations

The Man in the Straw Hat

1. Before the Curtain

I WAS NEVER meant to be an artiste.

And as I begin the story of my life I am more than ever impressed by this fact.

I wasn't meant to be an entertainer because, as the ninth child of the wife of an artisan, I was expected, like my brothers and all the other boys of my quarter, to learn a trade as soon as I had received my primary school certificate.

Apprentice, assistant, then workman: that was my normal course. For certainly there wasn't any artistic precedent in my family.

My father, Victor Charles Chevalier, was a house painter and a drunk. And my mother was Josephine Chevalier, a lace maker, a saintly woman who had brought ten children into the world. But only three of us were still living, my brother Charles, my brother Paul, and me, the youngest.

Now my older brother, Charles, had followed my father's trade, house painting, but my younger brother,

Paul, who was more gentle and refined, had taken up metal engraving.

When I compare my lack of education and culture and my unusual style of entertaining to that of other men in my profession, I am astonished that I have got by so nicely.

I've been very lucky all right. Because for half a century, with almost no voice, I have been able to attract and then hold the interest of the French public, the most changeable and sensitive audience in the whole world. It doesn't make any sense, does it?

You must not expect my story to be sensational. But I hope you will agree that I have come quite a way in the last fifty years from my childhood in Ménilmontant, when my greatest ambition was to earn my own soup and bread without owing anything to anyone.

2. Ménilmontant

I WAS BORN on the twelfth of September, 1888, at 29 Rue du Retrait, at the top of a hill. But I don't remember anything about my early childhood in this street. For, as you already know, I was the smallest of our family which consisted of my mother, my father, my two brothers, and myself.

Anyway, by the time I was old enough to know what was going on, we were living crowded on top of one another in a tiny two-room apartment at 15 Rue Julien Lacroix, still in Ménilmontant. I must explain that the Rue Julien Lacroix is a long, rather narrow street, running from the Rue Ménilmontant to the Rue Belleville.

Belleville and Ménilmontant belong to the same arrondissement, or district, and are like Siamese twins, stuck one to the other. One side of the Rue de Belleville belongs to the 20th arrondissement of Paris while the sidewalk opposite ends the 19th.

Belleville, swarming and crowded, might be the capital of the outskirts of Paris. There are a lot of workingmen in Belleville, but there are also many other kinds of people. A good, honest fellow will live next door to the lowest pimp. And respectable housewives line up at the baker's behind streetwalkers.

It is not necessary to put signs on the houses, as they do in the Casbah of Algiers, to show which is an honest household. Everyone knows everyone else, and one lives and lets live, except—except at nightfall, when the alleys are deserted and when the few open bars look like dens of cutthroats.

It is then that the late passer-by is in danger and the cheerful name "Belleville" suddenly takes on a dramatic ring. The Siamese sister, Ménilmontant, has a little of this inconsistency, but really very little.

Compared to Belleville, Ménilmontant is a bit like a calm, gentle parent and it has its poetic side. You find pleasing sights everywhere, from the Boulevard de Ménilmontant up to the Rue des Pyrénées.

Here live 90 per cent of the workingmen, the true artisans, the humble people who represent the real backbone. At one time or another I suppose I have sung of Ménilmontant in every possible key. And believe me, none of my songs has come more sincerely from the heart. How could it be otherwise?

In this little apartment on the Rue Julien Lacroix I first really began to appreciate all that my mother managed to do in the course of a day: housework, lace-making, cooking, laundry, and sewing for my father, my two brothers and me, the little one.

She was at it all day long. Usually when the evening meal was finished, the men, exhausted from their shop work, dozed off even before going to bed. But I can see Mamma now, the only moving figure in the half light of the little room, silently washing the dishes and then, still noiselessly, sewing by the turned-down lamp in a desperate attempt to finish a piece of work due the following day. And even then I felt instinctively that she was the most beautiful and the most heroic of our little family group.

Naturally the first part of my childhood is confused in

my memory. Some things are clear, then there are blanks. I remember, for example, that as soon as I could walk and talk I helped the family by running errands. They sent me to buy chops or "beefsteaks" at the horse butcher on the Rue Ménilmontant, or to buy a loaf of bread at the bakery at the corner of the Rue des Maronites near by. Sometimes I was asked to go to the dairy across the way and get butter (a quarter of a pound at a time for economy), eggs, or cheese. But I preferred the butcher and the baker because the butcher always tipped me with a morsel of horse-meat sausage, and the baker handed me a free stale roll, left over from the day before. However the dairy woman gave exact weight. Apparently my youthful charm had no effect on her because she never let herself be softened by my surprised and reproachful expression.

As for wine, my father brought that home inside himself. He filled up at all the saloons on the way between the place where he worked and the house where we waited for the evening meal.

It is only fair to say that Father did have the reputation of being a very good worker and that he was undeniably an honest and a good man. Still he was totally dominated by "the bottle" and this weakness caused Mamma much sorrow. And I used to find her weeping silently without complaint or explanation, in a corner of our apartment.

But small as I was, still I managed now and then to pick up a few sous for myself. Sometimes as I played in the street with the other kids, a strange man would signal to me.

Then leading me away from my friends he would ask me in a trembling voice to carry a letter to such and such a woman who lived near by in such and such a house on such and such a floor. Then I was expected to bring back an answer to the wretched fellow. He must have been a lover or a husband who was begging his lady to return after a quarrel. The poor fellow would give me a sou to pay for my share in his private life. When he was feeling particularly low, and misery twisted his features, he might give me two sous. Then I would run a little faster and do my best to bring him a hopeful answer.

What did I do with all this money? Well, I soon acquired two vices—almond sugar plums and two-for-a-penny cigarettes. After I had run a lot of errands, I bought myself so many almond sugar plums that my stomach felt cemented with almonds. They made me sickish and congested. Then in a secret hiding place I'd indulge in an orgy of smoking—two cigarettes, one after the other.

It did not take the reaction long to set in: cold sweats and dizziness, with the usual results! I had to go to bed and there Mamma's uneasy face would weave strangely before my troubled eyes.

Soon I was entered in the free Catholic school on the Rue Boyer to start learning to read and write. There, in an atmosphere entirely new to me, in the midst of other little animals of my own age, I quickly learned that the strongest are often the meanest.

In fact, on my very first day of school the older children lit into me. It was during recess in the courtyard that they shouted:

"Take a look at him, will you—the kid with the big head!"

I had, it is true, a head too big for my small body. But could I help that?

"What is the matter with my big head—eh, prune skin?" I was already learning the art of repartee.

"Ah! Big Head. Ah! Big Head. Ah! Big Head!"

The group around me grew. The crowd of schoolboys became ugly. They pushed me. One lad pulled my hair. Another kicked my backside. Now I was shaking all over. I couldn't understand it. I had done nothing wrong— what did they have against me, all these strangers?

Revolting blindly against such unjustice, I suddenly let out such a yelp that the voices ceased. And now all the eyes in all these frightful faces were fixed on me.

I had become wild, really wild! Without knowing how to fight I struck out like a crazy man, straight in front of me. I was transformed into a regular machine of fury and despair.

A little waif (apparently an innocent bystander—but what of that?) caught my fist on his nose, my head on his chin, and my foot between his legs. He fell down sobbing. I turned around, livid. I must have been a horrible sight, for my attackers quickly scattered. When the bell rang calling us back to class I felt that, although my knees were shaking with emotion and although I had been guided by fear rather than courage, I had done the right thing in a tough spot.

After this day my reputation as a bully was established and I never again had to prove my physical superiority.

But one week later, mind you, I was a choir boy! The curate, who had noticed that I had a nice little face (why, yes, I was very cute!) asked me if I'd like to be a choir boy at mass. A choir boy! Why, that was my dream because of the costume, red cassock, and lace surplice. Some class!

Now I had to rehearse and work, and one fine day I made my debut at mass. I don't know just what happened. But as I entered the church I couldn't keep from stealing a glance at my pals in the choir. I was proud of the cassock and surplice. Though they were pretending to pray, one, then two, then three boys began to giggle as I advanced pompously down the aisle. A surge of smothered laughter began to drown out the ceremony. The curate threw me a furious look, for by now I was laughing too. The mass ended unsuccessfully and so did my career as a choir boy.

Just when I thought I was so chic and had pictured myself as progressing rapidly along this sacred path! And

8

I had an insane desire to be the censer bearer in the pro-
cession. You know, he's the one who carries the censer,
with a wave of incense above and a wave of incense behind.
I was sure I could manage all that and at the same time
look like an angel.

But that's another dream I shall never realize, unless
it comes to me later when it's the style for choir boys to
wear white beards.

I have another and different kind of memory of that
church. One day I stood in the square at the bottom of
the church steps and held onto the railing spellbound,
watching a wedding party which was descending in great
style. It was beautiful, grand, and so rich!

I stared, transfixed. And so I didn't notice that someone had leaned on the gate. Suddenly it closed and my
finger was in the crack. I screamed out loud and the bride
and groom nearly tripped on the steps in their fright.
Finally someone opened the gate, but by now the end of
my finger hung loose. A crowd gathered.

"We must take this little boy to Tenon Hospital!" someone said. "What's your name?"

"Maurice Chevalier."

"Where do your parents live?"

"Near here at 15 Rue Julien Lacroix."

I saw them running as in a nightmare. I felt faint.
They brought Mamma. She came without saying a word
and with a set expression on her face. Her poor cheeks

looked hollow. She called a cab. (She would have to work half a day to earn the price of the fare, thirty centimes.) Kissing me crazily, she hurried me to Tenon Hospital. Mon Dieu, I was ill, but mighty proud of the importance of my accident, and Mamma's grief, and the ride in the cab.

3. Sorrows of the Poor

THIS BANDAGED FINGER, that I had to hold up in the air for nearly a month so as to avoid congestion, was the fore-runner of a whole series of events, each more unfortunate than the preceding.

First came my father.

After several days of continual drunkenness and piti-ful scenes at home, one evening (I almost said one fine evening) we saw him slam the door as he staggered out never to return, abandoning his wife and three children.

I'll skip over, a little shamefully, Mamma's sadness and humility and the brave decision of my older brother, Charles, to make himself the head of the family. This idea was right and helpful and Charles played his role seriously for a while. In fact, he took it almost too seri-ously. He became so strict with me that, in the evening when my mother let me play in the church square with the other brats, I'd watch anxiously for his return. Then when he appeared at the corner of the Rue Ménilmontant and the Rue Julien Lacroix, I'd run as fast as my frightened little legs could carry me to get to the house before him. Charles became a sort of tyrant and found fault with everything. Finally one evening he hit me for almost no reason at all. This caused a harrowing scene between Mamma and him. After that the small amount of affection that I felt for Charles was replaced by a hope of revenge at a later day.

Another time, without any valid reason, he gratified his desire to dominate by hitting me again. Pale, and drawn to my full height, with clenched teeth I assured him that, if I were bigger, it wouldn't be so easy for him to bully me like this. I had hardly finished my sentence before another blow from Charles struck my head with such force that I fell over like a wooden soldier.

A child doesn't forget things like that.

But in time the role of father began to bore Charles, and finally one day he told Mamma that he was twenty years old and wanted to live his own life. He was in love and determined to get married. Apparently he had already proposed to the girl and been accepted. He made it clear that in the future we were not to count on his salary. Poor Mamma didn't even try to make him wait until Paul received a full-fledged workman's salary. Instead, hiding her grief behind an understanding smile, she accepted this second desertion docilely.

I am vague about just what followed. I guess Charles married the daughter of his boss, or maybe it was someone else. What difference does it make? Anyway he disappeared from our lives suddenly and completely. So from that time on, there were only three of us, Mamma, Paul, and me.

I mentioned that Paul was not yet a full-fledged worker and was earning, I think, only three francs a day. Obviously the three of us couldn't live on that. So poor Mamma, besides having her housework and the care of two children and her lace making, which was already ruining her eyes, now had to do housework for kind neighbors.

Allowing herself less and less sleep and stinting herself more and more, she finally became so weak that we had to send for the charity doctor. She was now so anemic that she was slowly going blind. The rims of her eyelids bled and she was so weak physically that she fainted several times nearly every day. With haggard eyes, and her body trembling with anguish, she heard the doctor order her to the charity hospital. He explained that she had waited too long and that now the treatment would take a number of weeks. The doctor said that she would have to leave her children behind. Bravely the good woman tried once more to stifle her unhappiness. And, sobbing, she explained to Paul that he'd have to eat in the

cheap restaurant downstairs, and that he must be a good
boy. Then suddenly stiffening she pointed to me, "And
who will take care of *him*? Who will feed *him*?"

Gently the doctor told her about a large institution on
the Rue Denfert Rochereau called "The Children's Aid"
where were gathered all the abandoned children and the
unlucky ones whose mothers could not care for them. It
was quickly arranged for a neighbor to take me there that
very day with a certificate from the doctor demanding immediate admission. At this point my poor mother threw
herself upon me and our embrace lasted a long time.
Finally she had to be torn away, and only then did my
childish mind slowly begin to realize that she was leaving.

Still I felt instinctively that I must be a brave boy and
not cry, at least when I could be seen. After all, I was
eight years old now—no longer a baby! So, holding the
good neighbor's hand, this little poor child left for the
Children's Aid. That institution was located far from
Ménilmontant and so we had a long trip on the bus. We
crossed most of Paris and I found that entertaining, accustomed as I was to the monotony of one street and to
a very confined daily routine.

At long last we got off before a severe and imposing entrance over which we read the inscription, "Alms House
of the Children's Aid."

I looked to right and left. The depressing high, gray
buildings warned me that life is not all play.

The door opened. My neighbor explained my case and

showed the certificate. She tried to smile and then, after patting me on the back, she left. The attendant took me into a room where three other little waifs were waiting too. I looked at them round-eyed, realizing for the first time that other people also had troubles. Soon it was my turn to go to the office. I gritted my teeth. They put a little blue necklace on me that had a tag with a number engraved on it. They put a uniform over my arm, navy blue trousers, a blue shirt, and clean underwear. Then they washed me thoroughly with soap and water, and soon I looked just like all the other poor kids.

Our building contained boys of all sizes, small, medium, and large. The girls were in the building opposite.

Being eight, I belonged to the middle-aged group. However I regarded my fellow inmates with suspicion. I felt like a rabbit thrown into a cage with a lot of strange rabbits. But one kid, more sensitive and affectionate than the others, was nice to me now.

"Your mother will soon be well," he said. "You'll see. We are happy here and we have good white beds that smell of lavender. We eat well and we even get dessert!"

I learned that some of these wretched children were so unhappy at home that they sobbed when a relative came to take them back. But I had been happy with my dear mother, so now I clenched my fists in my pockets trying to keep back my tears. While the others went to sleep in the dormitory at night, I prayed, "Our Father who art in heaven, cure Mamma quickly."

And, thank the Lord, my wish finally came true. One day an orderly called my name at recess. "They are here for you," he said, "Go and change. Your mother is well again."

I ran as fast as I could, stumbling in my eagerness.

Everything seemed like a dream. The same kind neighbor who had brought me was waiting in the office near the exit with papers in hand.

I stared at her, not daring to believe it.

But, it was true. We went out in the street and again took the bus. This time, however, I was not interested in the trip across Paris. Just one face kept appearing before my eyes. I was going to see Her and touch Her again. How my heart beat!

At last we were at the Rue Julien Lacroix! There was number 15! I climbed the stairs three at a time. I entered our flat and saw her sitting there with outstretched arms, still weak and pale.

I went straight to the crook in her shoulder and there, where I had often gone to sleep, I was happy again.

Now I really understood the meaning of the word "Mamma."

4. The Chevalier Brothers

WE DIDN'T HAVE much fun in the Chevalier family! That's what you are thinking, isn't it? I cannot contradict you— I agree! All the same I must tell things as they happened.

I ask you—do you know anybody whose life has been gay and cheery from beginning to end?

Well, Mamma was back from the hospital and Paul had become head of the family. We had a hard time for several weeks, but one Saturday evening we had a happy surprise. Paul, as a reward for his good work (you remember that he was a metal engraver), was going to be raised, sooner than expected, to the salary of a skilled workman. He would get seven francs a day. So the next Saturday he'd bring home forty-two francs for a week's work!

This fortune, added to what Mamma earned so painfully at lace making, would bring us a little ease for the first time. After all our ups and downs we three were about to find a little happiness.

Paul was very loving and very conscientious and brought home his pay faithfully. Mamma added her profits, and she was feeling fine again now. Everything was going so well that each Sunday Paul and I bought an armful of flowers for our Louque. The "Louque" is what we decided to call her, and even if you were to break my nose in eleven places, I couldn't explain that nickname. It doesn't mean anything. Mamma belonged to us and she was our Louque and that was that.

A new life began at 15 Rue Julien Lacroix: to mark our rise in the world, we changed apartments. We moved from the third floor down to the first, with a window on the street, if you please! We had saved up a little money, so we moved in style with new flowered wallpaper and both rooms freshly painted.

Things got better and better. I now went to the public school on Rue Julien Lacroix, just a hundred yards from the house.

Having more time and leisure for diversions, every Saturday, and often on Sunday, too, we set out with the Louque, like three pals, to attend either the Palais du Travail or the Cirque d'Hiver or the Concert du Commerce or the Cirque Medrano.

I was fascinated by certain singers and by some of the acrobatic acts as well. Especially did I envy the boys who could land on their feet after doing backward somersaults from each other's heads.

At home I dreamed about this over and over again. I became all worked up over the lights and the applauding audience and the thought of the sous I could earn. In fact, I was crazy to become an acrobat myself.

I was now nine years old. After school, with the other

kids of our arrondissement, I'd practice somersaults and balancing acts on the sandpiles of the Rue Sorbier. I tried to describe to my pals the feats of the acrobats whom I had seen at the circus.

Later on I learned how professional acrobats train their children to do these dangerous forward and backward somersaults. A long bar is held by two men and the child must somesault around it dozens of times before he is allowed to go it alone.

Of course we kids knew nothing of these professional methods. But what did we care! We just went right at it.

"I bet you can't do a forward somersault in the air!"

"I bet I can."

And the daring one would land on his back, or his behind, or even on his head. It was because of these falls that we stuck to the sandpiles.

However, bruised and battered though we were, we improved from day to day. Crowds always gathered about us, and if one of us was successful, they applauded him enthusiastically.

I don't know if it was fanaticism or the hope of earning money that made me go at it harder than the others. But anyway I soon acquired the reputation of being the best acrobat in the neighborhood. Not wishing to lose my status, the minute school was out I ran like a racehorse to our improvised outdoor gymnasium.

Neighbors told Mamma of my unexpected bent. I begged her to let me alone. And she realized that it was better to amuse myself like this than to join up with the street gangs who sought me out because I was "a good fighter."

Sitting at the table in the evening between Mamma and Paul, who was now sixteen, I talked about nothing but acrobatics. The acts that we had applauded at the circus had definitely turned my head.

Soon Paul too caught the bug and we started to plan an act of our own. We greatly admired the billboards that we studied each week end; the printed notices with English titles such as "Walton Brothers," "Fernandis Brothers," and this kind of "Brothers" and that kind of "Brothers."

We thought that "Brothers" was a first name like Louis or Jules, and only later on did we learn that "brothers" was the English word for *frères*.

Then we got an idea. After searching and searching we finally found a printer who had some old lithographs of two men in tights. On top of them shone the glamorous name "Martinon Brothers."

Paul, who was very clever with his hands, quickly made up some strips to paste over the name Martinon. Now we were the proud owners of a lot of posters reading "Chevalier Brothers."

We stuck one up in our bedroom and marveled at the effect, trying to impress the Louque with what we considered a stroke of genius.

We were going to put on such a wonderful "brothers"

act! We'd be a huge success! We were going to earn so much money! Mamma smiled and pretended to agree that it was perfectly possible, provided that Paul didn't leave his workshop and that I kept up my school work.

We had our posters. That seemed to us the main thing. Now all we had to do was perfect the act—a mere trifle.

Paul was to be the anchor man. I would do the somersaults and the balancing stunts.

We discovered the Arras Gymnasium on the Rue Ménil-montant. You could stay there as long as you wanted for five sous. Young wrestlers went there to improve their muscles with weight lifting. And acrobats came to keep in form. This was our meat. Every evening after work Paul met me there and we rehearsed different routines that we had dreamed up. We spent every Sunday and holiday there too.

The first evening that Paul and I went to the gymnasium we were somewhat nonplused by all the people. There were amateurs practicing weight lifting, acrobats rehearsing new stunts, and wrestlers heaving and groaning. In this company we hardly dared put on our tights, but we finally made up our minds to it.

Paul wanted to improve his muscles, so he began to imitate the weight lifters, trying to look nonchalant as he did so. All of them went through just about the same gyrations. First, with sad and far-away expressions, they'd get into position behind the weights. Then, heaving sighs, of which I didn't understand the significance, they'd scratch at the sawdust on the floor with their feet like dogs.

All of these preparations were made slowly and with the most desolate expression in the world. Then, when they'd decided that there was no other possible way of improving the position of the weight, they'd raise their trousers slightly and move their torsos a bit as if to prepare everything just so. Finally, with the expression of a desperate man leaping from a bridge to end his life, they'd pounce at the weights like a lion at its prey.

But all that was just the start. The caliber of the athlete really showed up in his ability to lift the weight above the shoulder in one try.

Those who could not lift the weight higher than their chests, wriggled their bodies and rolled their eyes wildly. And we couldn't help laughing at them.

Others, who could only get the weight as high as their shoulders seemed to suffer even more horribly. Their veins stood way out and they appeared to be on the verge of suffocation. We wondered why they ever chose this kind of martyrdom as a recreation.

Among these athletes were a few powerful fellows who found all of this as easy as lighting a match.

In an offhand manner, these wonder boys would turn to one of their perspiring neighbors and ask, "What did you say? That weighs how much? Fifty pounds? Well, well, let's see—hup! Why, that's nothing at all! Bring me a heavier one, I beg of you."

21

Now, after taking a good look at these characters, Paul chose a twenty-pound dumbbell and tried to lift it in the air. For the first time I noticed that he was extremely bow-legged. And he looked so thin beside these sturdy men with their thick arms and large chests! Perhaps I shouldn't try to make him into a "Brother" after all. Seeing him like that my throat choked up and I suddenly wanted to cry.

My sudden discouragement was mixed with a great wave of affection for Paul. Perhaps my enthusiasm had started us down a road that we couldn't travel very far.

But I didn't confide these forebodings to my brother. Instead I began to climb onto his shoulders. I've always felt that my balancing on his head caused his Adam's apple to become so well developed.

After a short time I had to admit to myself that I didn't have enough strength in my arms or in my legs either. I couldn't spring high enough. Instead of "getting up" to sixty or seventy inches from the floor, I had to somer-sault in the air almost at floor level.

God knows I tried. My stubbornness kept us at it day after day. But no one at the Arras Gymnasium thought we were good enough to make the Palais du Travail as the "Chevalier Brothers."

Finally the date of my school graduation examinations arrived and, discouraged physically and mentally, I had the happy surprise of succeeding where I had expected to fail miserably. I was ten and a half years old, school was over, and now I had to learn a trade.

5. First Song

THE FAMILY held council around the table to decide what profession I should take up. For me the answer was simple! I wanted to be an acrobat. But Mamma and Paul didn't think that a suitable profession, and I had to make another choice.

So I decided that I'd be least unhappy near Paul in his workshop. And we agreed that Paul should ask his foreman to take me on as an apprentice engraver. This was arranged, and I started in the workshop at 14 Rue Vertbois, near the Place de la République, at ten sous a day.

From the very first week I felt that I'd never make a good metal engraver. My mind was entirely on plans for the stage and the circus ring. And I finally worked Paul up to renting a little fifteen-foot plot at the end of Belleville. This was where workingmen spent their Sundays growing vegetables. But we spaded up the ground to soften it for our gymnastics. The space cost twenty francs a year. This was a good deal cheaper than going to the Arras every day.

In the evening, after our day at the workshop, we had to trudge for a good hour to reach our "gymnasium." Then we'd practice our stunts alone. We had a few small accidents. I fell and sprained my foot. Paul's ear was painfully torn when my foot slipped while I was trying to stand on his head. We weren't able to keep at it for long, and on reaching home we would be weak with fatigue.

Paul's boss soon discovered that my mind was not on my work, and one Saturday I came home with the news of my discharge. I was not to return on Monday. That meant seventy sous less each week. Mamma took the blow well and consoled me by saying that I'd certainly find other work on Monday.

That same day my kind brother Paul told me that he would have to quit the team of "Chevalier Brothers." Being an anchor man at night after working as a metal engraver all day was too much. The poor kid had already lost weight and his Adam's apple had become greatly enlarged.

Everything seemed to go wrong for me. But, stubbornly, I determined to find out once and for all whether or not I was good enough to become an acrobat.

When I applied at the Cirque they took me on trial, without salary, as part of an acrobatic trio. I was to be the one who balances on the head of the man who was already balanced on the head of the anchor man. I was the top man! From this position I must leap into the air in a somersault, while the second fellow jumped to the floor. Then I would land on the head of the anchor man.

One day while we were practicing this stunt my foot

slipped. It was frightful! With all the force of my leap my chin, then my nose, struck the back of the man's head. They picked me up in a faint, with my face all bloody. My mother said that enough was enough. She was sure that some day I'd be crippled in this cruel profession.

I, too, was pretty discouraged. So, abandoning my dreams of fame, I began to look for a job. As I went to the various addresses that I'd found among the want ads posted near the streetcar in Temple, a new hope began to form in my mind. If I couldn't become an acrobat, how about being a singer? Except for the ones we had heard at the Commerce and the Palais du Travail, most of them, especially the comedians, did not have much of a voice. If I put myself to it seriously, why couldn't I do as well as that peasant comedian, Carlos, or that old trouper Mulhéry? O.K.! I had a new bug, and, dropping my old passion like a faded vamp, I started to plan for my debut as a comic singer. But I decided not to mention it to Mamma until later when I was sure of myself. I would be an apprentice at whatever she and Paul wished, but I would also learn some songs.

I won't try to list all of the trades that I tackled after this. I was fired every two weeks. First I was a carpenter and joiner. They thought I spent too much time in the "W.C.," where I'd stand on the toilet seat and sing to an imaginary audience.

Then I was an electrician. They let me go because I was slow on errands. I watched out for all the music shops and stood open-mouthed reading the titles and learning the names of the great singers who were much too important to come to Ménilmontant.

As a doll painter I was sacked because I couldn't paint the doll faces according to directions. I had seen the notices of Mayol, Polin, and Dranem. As I thought of them constantly while I worked, the dolls took on the faces of these popular artists.

Being clerk for a paint merchant suited me better, for in this job I was allowed to wait on the customers. I was eleven and a half now and enjoyed teasing my boss who, although in his fifties, was hardly any taller than I was. When a customer entered I would greet him or her politely with "What do you wish, my little friend?" or, "May I serve you, little girl?"

Nine times out of ten the customers to whom I spoke were much older and bigger than I, and it was because of their complaints that I was dismissed. That day my boss took pleasure in assuring me that I'd always be "a little shrimp."

I earned more money making thumbtacks. This was an unskilled trade, and I could turn out tacks quickly and easily. My work went like this: I was seated before a press. At my left were boxes of unformed tacks. With my left hand I fed them one by one into a kind of little mould, and with my right I bore down on their heads with the press. If I was in good form, I could turn out a thumbtack with two blows.

I was paid by the thousand tacks at the end of the week, and in good weeks I brought home as much as ten francs. But once again my mind began to wander and my receipts dwindled to eight francs, and then to six.

The son of the firm was a damned nuisance. He'd come up behind me a dozen times a day to inspect my work. Of course it was never right, and each time he'd have to show me how it should be done. Besides all this, his putrid breath made me sick.

One day my absent-mindedness got me into trouble. As I was thinking of anything but the tack industry, I left my hand on the mold as I came down with the hammer. I let out a yell! The other workers gathered around. My finger hung completely crushed.

Again they sent for Mamma who took me to the hospital —here we go again!

For several weeks now I had been attending an amateur show in the back room of the Café des Trois Lions on the Boulevard de Ménilmontant. It was open Saturday and Sunday evenings and we went on Saturdays. The admission price was twenty-five centimes, which included refreshments. The enthusiastic audience was mostly made up of workingmen.

There we heard a young clock maker named Georgel, who sang the songs of Mayol, and a comedian after the style of Dranem, named Brigham, and an imitator of Polin named Léon D. These three showed real promise. Some of the others were so dreadful that I won't mention them.

Georgel, the star of Les Trois Lions, was thickset and had an attractive face. He had a sweet voice and was amazingly restrained for an amateur.

Leon D. was a tall, rather thin fellow. He didn't look at all like Polin, whose style he copied. But he had such a pleasant voice and such a charming face that the women in the audience had a hard time choosing between him and Georgel.

Brigham's voice was hoarse and he was very funny. His was the subtle wit of a plumber, which perfectly suited this particular audience.

Then on Sunday evenings we Chevaliers went to the Palais du Travail, where Carlos and Mulhéry were my idols.

I was crazy about Carlos' costume. He wore a comical little hat over a bright cotton cap set backwards on his head. He sported very loud striped trousers, wooden shoes, a blue shirt embroidered in white, and huge white gloves. Under one arm he carried a basket from which peeped a duck's head. Under the other was a large umbrella.

I had already bought two of Carlos' folk songs, "V'la les Croquants" (Here Come the Clodhoppers) and "Youp Youp Larifla." So I went to the Place du Temple and bought a "get-up" like his. Mamma considered this a harmless pastime. She refitted and sewed and pressed my things, never dreaming that I would really use them.

I secretly practiced my two songs day and night, at

home, on the street and at the tack factory. I tried to mimic the gestures of Carlos.

It was at this point that I smashed my finger.

During the period of enforced idleness I came to a courageous decision. Approaching the owner of Les Trois Lions I asked him if I could sing my two songs on the following Saturday. With my large white gloves no one would see my bandaged finger.

The proprietor looked at me in astonishment. I was twelve years old and, as I have said, small for my age. He asked me if I lived in that arrondissement and if my parents knew of this step. When I assured him that they did, he invited me to come with my paraphernalia at eight o'clock Saturday evening. In payment I was to get a cup of coffee.

Wild with joy I relayed the good news to Mamma and Paul. They laughed and promised to attend my debut as an amateur.

On the fatal evening I arrived with the Louque and Paul, who bought two tickets. Then behind the flowered curtain I sorted my costume before the amused eyes of the stars. I only came up about to their belly button. After dressing, and borrowing makeup, I smeared my nose and cheeks with rouge.

When I handed my music to the pianist he asked in what key I would sing. That was a silly question!

"In any key you want," I answered.

My ignorance was equaled only by my determination. He asked me if I was ready. I should say I was!

The pianist began "V'la les Croquants" and I stepped forth in all my peasant garb.

Here is the song:

> *I had come to Paris*
> *The capital to see.*
> *My eyes were astonished,*
> *Unequaled my glee.*
> *Indeed I was not alone,*
> *I brought with me*
> *All kinds of natives from my village,*
> *My friends and family.*

CHORUS

> *My father,*
> *My mother,*
> *My sister, my cousin, my brother,*
> *Cath'rine,*
> *Jacqu'line,*
> *My uncle, my godfather and my aunt so fair,*
> *Théophile, Androche Honoré,*
> *Barnabé and Apolinaire.*

At first the people were surprised to see a child decked out like this. Then they began to smile at my determination. Feeling I had made a good start, I took myself in hand and stared at a point on the ceiling so that I could

30

put my whole mind on my song. I heard the piano all right, but for some reason we didn't seem to be entirely in accord. I bawled out my song as loudly as I could. Out of the corner of my eye I could see the pianist rise up as he played. They called to me from behind the scene but nothing could stop me now.

At the end of the verse and the chorus everyone in the room was laughing. The men slapped their thighs and the women were in hysterics. What a success! Still staring at the ceiling I continued, shouting louder than ever.

I finished "V'la les Croquants" amid an undescribable ovation and left the floor. I found Georgel and Léon D. flopped on chairs mopping their eyes.

I wanted to go back and acknowledge my unheard-of triumph, but they restrained me. They explained that next time it would be a good thing for me to have a rehearsal with the pianist.

"Why?" I asked.

"Because, little boy, you have just sung your song three keys higher than the accompaniment. The people were laughing at the way you forced your voice."

I fell from the heights. I had thought I was such a hit and now I had to admit to myself that the enthusiasm of the audience was not what it had seemed.

I was very sad as I returned home with Mamma and Paul. But they couldn't help laughing at the thought of my little figure with the rouged face howling my three verses in the face of the gale. They consoled me by saying

31

that I'd do better tomorrow if I'd only keep on key with the pianist.

But anyway, for better or worse, I had made a start on the stage, before the public and all by myself!

6. *Apprentice Singer*

THAT MORNING everybody in the Rue Julien Lacroix was laughing at me. The whole place seemed to be doubled up with hands on hips. Last night's audience had started the rumor.

"I saw Mother Chevalier's child singing at the Trois Lions—*You* know, the little blockhead—" "What brass!" "You should have seen him! They couldn't stop him. He sang—and sang—in a small, shrill voice that kept cracking —and he stared at the ceiling the whole time like a blind man." "We were almost sick with laughter but it didn't bother that clown! He went on faster and louder. What a dunce he is!"

Sunday at the Trois Lions was just like Saturday, except that I was less hysterical. I had learned that I would not drop dead when I set foot on the stage. That was something, anyway!

Georgel and Léon D. (his family name was Delpierre) took pity on me and pointed out that it was absolutely necessary for the singer and the piano to function in the same key. They explained that although I had obviously made the public laugh it was not kind laughter and did not prove that I was "an artist."

Kind laughter—artist—these two expressions entered my receptive noggin that day never to leave it.

I realized that I could not just step out onto the stage and sing. If I was to be a real artist I would have to work at it. I thought over all this as I went about my errands for Mamma on Monday morning. All the storekeepers, knowing the news, asked questions. They seemed to serve me a little better than usual. The butcher gave me a better horsemeat sausage; the baker a fresh roll.

"Tell us how you happened to do it?" they asked. "Who advised you?" "Where did you learn all that?"

I didn't know the answer myself. I realized that I had had a lot of nerve and my mind was in a whirl now.

But at least I had made a start and the hardest part was over. That was the main thing. From tomorrow on I just had to sing better.

We went to the Concert de Commerce in the Faubourg du Temple for the Sunday matinee. Verner, the manager, was himself a comic actor. Then there was a rough kind of fellow named Barock who was a monologuist. He was a pillar of the suburban cafés and was well liked by the workingmen. He lisped, drank to excess, and his slangy

33

jokes were mostly extemporaneous. At the end of the show he and the owner regularly put on an act. But they rehearsed only the beginning and the end. All the rest was improvised and I remember it as being hilarious.

Now the neighborhood boys had a crush on a girl named Valdina. She was tall and statuesque and sang what we called "Les Gommeuses" (The Mashers). She wore a large English-style hat and a very short and lowcut dress. You got a good view of her legs and her imposing bosom.

With a switch in her hand she paced back and forth on the stage, flashing her jewels and inspiring desire in every male in the room. She had a habit of leaning over innocently to speak to the pianist in the orchestra and of remaining bent over long enough for all of the males in the room to have a good look at her large bosom.

She was the girl of their dreams, but she scared me. She was too imposing, too important. If she'd ever even touched my cheek I'd have run like hell.

Still, although I was only a baby, my life was already complicated by a couple of females.

There was a little girl about my age named Georgette who lived on the church square. Sometimes in the evening we would sit hand in hand without talking. I liked to think of her as "my girl."

Then there was Daudibert, the favorite commedienne of the Quartier, whom we had seen with Raoul Villet several times at the Belleville Folies. I was positively enchanted with this young woman, although she (unfortunately) never knew it. She had a charming face and a clear and sunny smile. Her figure was plump in just the right spots and it stirred me strangely. I'd wait for her after the Sunday matinee. And when she appeared in the street on the arms of the comedian and the tenor, Robert Spada, the Adonis of Belleville, I would follow them to the door of the little restaurant where they went for dinner. I'd wait outside while they dined, then follow them back to the artist's entrance. And I'd return to 15 Rue Julien Lacroix completely overcome with emotion.

So, although the attractive Valdina upset the lives of all the gay blades of Belleville and Ménilmontant, she got nowhere with me. My body and soul belonged to Georgette and Daudibert.

At the Concert de Commerce there was also a young man of about twenty who sang as a "curtain raiser." Two or three acts later he appeared again. Besides these two songs, he helped the star to change backstage and ended the evening with a small role in the one-act play in which Verner and Barock improvised the most surprising nonsense. Then, too, he prompted if an artist needed help. In fact he did everything but sweep out the place. This fellow's name was Boucot. He was very dark and rather short and his head was a little too large for his body. His serious face lent little gaiety to his cavernous voice.

As an opener he appeared in a black suit and sang Mayol's song:

> *It was hardly a love affair.*
> *I plucked only one little flower in May,*
> *But it cost me six francs*
> *Though I was her lover for just a day.*

As Boucot couldn't afford pumps, which were then the fashion, he substituted shiny rubbers over his shoes. Both he and the audience considered this the height of elegance. (People weren't too fussy in Belleville.) Boucot had a way of sticking out his tongue after each sentence. His body seemed as stiff as a poker. And all in all I must admit his first appearance on the stage was pretty repulsive.

But when Boucot reappeared as a comedian, the change was extraordinary. This boy, who had been so grotesque a few moments before, now really let himself go and the audience gave him a big hand. He certainly was a funny sight. His suit was too tight on his thin little body. His large face was painted red and white under a hat that was too small. And, aided by his solemn voice, he made an irresistible buffoon. Yes sir, Boucot was the hit of the evening, no matter what star might be there. I thought he was wonderful.

At the end of the Sunday matinee I found the courage to speak to him and he kindly asked me if I, too, was a singer.

"Yes, M'sieur Boucot," I answered, "And I know that you live with your parents on the Rue Lepage, right next to the Rue Julien Lacroix where my mother, my brother, and I have our apartment. You are lucky, M'sieur Boucot, to sing in a real show with real artists. I am only an amateur, and in a few days, when my finger is healed, I'll have to go back to work at the shop."

I can't say that we became real friends, but Boucot did allow me to see him and to go to his home. Sometimes we went together to the Buttes Chaumont where he painted landscapes. I would sit quietly near by and wonder how he could find pleasure in anything but singing.

Once a week he put on a hat and his best coat with a velvet collar. He was bound for the music editors in Saint Martin and Saint Denis to get novelties for his next program.

Wanting to make the most of the few days left until my finger healed, I asked Boucot to let me "go down" into Paris with him. I was all excited at the thought of seeing the editors and the rehearsal rooms where the artists learned new songs. Boucot agreed, somewhat condescendingly, and one fine day, after lunch, we dressed up and went down together.

That was a great day for me. I got to see all of the places where they composed the popular refrains that haunted my mind.

Kindly, and rather proud of his role as Cicerone, Boucot took me everywhere. We went to Christiné, the genius of popular songs who wrote the great hits of Mayol, Polin, and Dranem. We went to Gramet, who wrote and published comic monologues, and to Benoit, and Jouve, and

37

Krier. I stared at the women with whom Boucot talked, but he didn't even introduce me.

He pointed out Mayol, prince of singers of the period, as he came out of Christiné's office. Mayol had a very pleasant face. He was portly and well groomed. His blond hair stuck out in waves from behind the derby that he wore well forward on his head. On his cane was a huge silver knob. He looked rich, well fed, and sure of himself.

As he said good-bye to the editor's clerk, his eyes wandered first to Boucot and then to me. He raised his eyebrows in surprise at the sight of this little kid staring at him as if he were something holy.

He walked slowly toward me while speaking to Boucot: "You're an artist?" he asked.

"Yes, Monsieur Mayol," answered Boucot. "Sometimes I sing your songs."

"And the boy?"

"He also sings, Monsieur Mayol, as an amateur. He's only twelve years old."

Mayol looked at me kindly, and if I hadn't hung on tighter to Boucot's arm I'm sure I would have fainted with excitement.

Then, without asking my name, Mayol smiled sweetly and left the building with a kind of graceful, mincing gait. Now my afternoon was complete, and so I begged Boucot to go back "up to" Ménilmontant. I dreamt all night of actors and song sheets and posters. And in the morning I awoke absolutely exhausted.

Several days later I had to return to the thumbtack prison and make thumbtacks all day long. My mind was never on my work. It was a miracle that in the next few days I didn't smash all my fingers in the machine. I made endless trips to the "W.C.," which had now become my "rehearsal room."

I sang softly in there, so as not to be heard, and bowed to imaginary applause. But after a while I had to come out and face the suspicious owners and the stifled laughter of the other workers. I tried to look upset and haggard as though I had been sick. And I was foolish enough to think that I could get away with this day after day.

Every Saturday and Sunday I went back to Les Trois Lions. My success was not as noisy as on the evening of my debut, but I was getting better. I was no longer nervous and could now look elsewhere than the ceiling. Most important of all, I now sang in the same key with the piano.

These two evenings each week were heaven to me. Without them I would not have had the heart to return each Monday to my thumbtack tomb.

Then for several weeks I had to give up Les Trois Lions. Necessary repairs and redecorating forced the café to close. Our little troupe of amateurs would have to carry on somewhere else during this period. Finally we found a little café in Rue Popincourt in the eleventh arrondissement where they would let us sing for several weeks.

Pretentiously we called our new show "The Popincourt

Follies." But I must admit that our debut was discouraging. At Les Trois Lions we had a nice following of workingmen who knew us all. But no one here in the eleventh arrondissement had even heard of us. And no one was tempted by the hand-drawn notices with which we plastered the windows of the café.

The first Saturday we sang before eleven or twelve people scattered around the dark and smoky room. These were working-class couples too, but most of them were drunk. The men were down at the heel and they driveled and belched. The women were in the same state and crying to boot because their drunken husbands had already spent most of their week's wages in the one evening. The charming songs of Georgel and Leon D. and the jokes of Brigham were lost on that evil-smelling room.

I sensed that the glassy eyes of "our public" did not even see me as I sang. For they never once stopped drinking or crying or belching.

At the end of the evening we artistes drank to our friendship at the bar. But a shout from Brigham awoke us from our despair.

"Look, boy, there's a spider in my glass!" In truth a fat spider seemed to be enjoying a bath in the Picon.

"What have we here?" shouted Brigham. "Why, this isn't the Popincourt Follies, this must be the Spider Follies!"

We returned to Belleville discussing our failure and I didn't see our little troupe again for some time.

On the Rue Ménilmontant there was a tobacco concern with a large banquet room in the rear. They announced the opening for the following Saturday of a show, half amateur and half professional, called the "Elysée Ménilmontant." On the strength of my reputation at Les Trois Lions, if you please, they engaged me at sight—but still without pay.

That Saturday my luck took a turn for the better.

7. *Artiste!*

ON THE OPENING DAY of the Elysée Ménilmontant the whole neighborhood was humming;

"Good morning, Madame Duval, are you going to the show?"

"Yes, Monsieur Lacroix, it should be good. Some real professionals are coming all the way from Lake Saint Fargeau by bus."

"Be careful you don't fall in love with the beautiful Yvonne de Verlac."

"Who's this 'Little Chevalier'?"

"I think he's a local boy. They say he's very funny for his age."

That evening through a hole in the curtain Paul and I watched the spectators take their places. Mamma was there with a neighbor. She looked around proudly as if the whole crowd must know that she was the mother of one of the performers. I felt that I must do my best for my adored Louque.

There was an atmosphere of good humor in that room. During my short time as an amateur I had now seen three kinds of audience: the laughing, noisy, friendly workmen at Les Trois Lions, the unspeakable type of the Spider Follies, and the audience at L'Elysée Ménilmontant which was by far the most sensitive and well behaved of the three.

The manager placed me near the end of the program, just before the star. First some amateurs came on. They were not nearly so good as our troupe at Les Trois Lions. Then Léger, the hunchback, sang and danced. He was a great success. And Yvonne de Verlac enchanted the men with her clever songs. After this Léger and Yvonne did a number together which brought down the house. The crowd was thoroughly enjoying the evening.

Then they announced "Little Chevalier" and I made my entrance. They laughed and applauded and there were murmurs of "Oh, isn't he small!" and "But he's only a child!"

I looked at the Louque and saw that her lips were trembling. Turning, I could see Paul nervously standing close

42

by in the wing. I looked at Mamma again with an encouraging smile. Then I began!

For the first time since my debut I felt that I had a real command of the audience. At the end they applauded and called me back. I was so excited that I did not even see Paul when he hugged me. They kept on clapping. What could I do? I didn't know any more songs.

"Thank the audience, little one," said the manager, "And tell them that Gilbert, the 'Mayol of Tourelles,' will sing next."

I did this and took my place backstage to admire the star.

The great Mayol was such a success at this time that each district of Paris had a favorite who sang his songs. He might be called the "Mayol of Tourelles," the "Mayol of Grenelle," or some other species of Mayol.

Gilbert came on dressed in a black suit, with his hat well forward on his head. He was smooth shaven and a little overpowdered. He even minced onto the stage like Mayol.

In the wings I kept time to the snappy music of his song:

> *Little errand girls, keep your eyes open.*
> *Watch out for old gentlemen.*
> *It has a reason—that covetous eye*
> *On the turn of your neck as you go by.*
> *For a good dinner they will pay,*

And little gifts should not dismay,
And when they ask for more send them away.

The audience loved "The Errand Girls' Polka" and asked for more. After singing "Folichonade," Gilbert cut his greatest figure with Fragson's popular hit, "Limping Love."

And I said to myself, seeing she was so nice,
"It is too bad that she limps like that, the poor girl."

I was thrilled to see a real professional close up. Followed by Paul, I went to my corner of the dressing room to pack my costume. There Gilbert, surrounded by admirers, was slowly putting on his overcoat and adjusting his white silk scarf.

He kept staring at me.

Intimidated beyond words, I didn't dare speak to him. But as I started to leave the dressing room he stopped me.

"I heard you a while ago, little one. How long have you been singing?" he asked.

I looked around, thinking he was probably speaking to someone else. Then, certain that he meant me, I stiffened and said:

"Only about six months, Monsieur. That's why I'm so self-conscious."

"And how much do they pay you here?" he asked kindly.

"Oh, nothing, Monsieur. Goodness! I'm happy that they let me come at all!"

He thought for a moment, then said, "Come to the Tourelles Casino tomorrow evening at eight o'clock with your music and your costume and I will ask the director for a public audition. If you please him, as I think you will, he'll ask you to sing there for a week or two at a fair price. If you don't make the grade, they'll give you a little something for your bus fare anyway. What can you lose?"

I opened my mouth to accept but not a word came out. Finally I swallowed two or three times noisily and stammered that I was very grateful.

When I returned Paul helped me to persuade the Louque that this audition was worth while. I lay awake that night thinking of all that had happened to me and resolved that I would work hard to prove my love for them both.

If I live to be a hundred and fifty I won't forget that Sunday evening in December, 1901. I arrived with Paul an hour ahead of time. The Casino was in darkness. The matinee was over and the performers were dining in a little restaurant near by. The doorman did not know about me and refused to let us in. Bundle in hand we paced up and down the Avenue Gambetta for three quarters of an hour.

The doors opened to the public at eight o'clock. At a quarter of eight we presented ourselves at the stage door. There Gilbert himself welcomed us and introduced me to the director, an old comedian named Rithier.

Rithier looked at me kindly but without confidence. I felt frightfully shy, but I was determined to go on that stage dressed as a peasant and sing my best. If I could only get a paid engagement I would be able to take home a few sous to the Louque.

Finally, shrugging his shoulders, Rithier said I could try. I would be number three. First came a woman, then a man, then me with my two songs.

The show began. The pianist, to whom I had explained my manner of singing, played two or three popular songs as an opening. We all joined in singing the familiar airs.

First the woman sang rather poorly. Then the comedian, Caron, was received by a tempest of laughter and bawdy jokes. He was repulsive. His voice cracked and his diction was indistinct. I suffered for him. But his songs were only a pretext for the exchange of wit with the audience that followed. He soon had them in stitches.

Gilbert explained to me that this rapid, brutal, and lashing repartee was Caron's strong point. He was known to be a constant drinker and always came on stage well fried and in a good humor.

When the storm of applause lessened the management put up a sign in large letters saying "Audition." It was my turn. The people had been laughing and shouting so noisily that my entrance went almost unnoticed. It took the audience several moments to recover and to adjust to my small size and my youth.

Several women applauded and a few men looked at me, but most of them were still under the spell of Caron. With the second song they began to pay more attention. Still their laughter was anemic, and when I left the stage I felt that I had failed. I expected that I would only get my carfare.

Then Rithier and Gilbert burst out with:

"Very good, little fellow! You please them. You'll have to work hard, but they think you are funny and courageous."

It takes plenty of courage, I thought to myself, to be gay unless you get applause. I couldn't say anything. I felt sure that they spoke to me out of pity.

"Listen, little fellow," said Rithier, "you begin next Thursday. We work four days a week: Thursday, Saturday, Sunday, and Monday. There are two shows an evening. How much do you want?"

Absolutely overcome I stuttered, "Whatever you say— I don't know."

"All right," said the director, "you stay two weeks. I'll give you twelve francs a week and three francs a day extra for practicing. If you learn new songs and if you're a success we'll have another talk—is that O.K.?"

By lowering his eyelids and nodding his head, my brother signaled that I should accept.

I made a rapid calculation. This would mean two francs more than my best weeks at the tack factory. So this meant no more factory. I would be free all day and, above all, I would be a professional singer!

Overcome with joy I accepted. Arm in arm Paul and I dashed home to the apartment in a state of wild enthusiasm.

Mamma, in her quiet, loving way, took in our excitement. Her expression said, "Since this is the way it is, we shall see."

"But," she insisted, "if you don't find an engagement after the Casino de Tourelles will you promise to return to the workshop?"

Boom—this was it! This was putting it up to me!

I soon had a slap in the face to balance this new happiness.

In the Faubourg du Temple, near Parmentier, was a men's hat shop. On the front were three large numbers, "3—6—9." In the window were displayed three grades of hats; one grade sold at nine francs, another at six francs, and a third at three francs. The shapes of the hats were the same, but the quality of the felt varied with the price.

There were derbies, and soft hats, and above all "Girondin" hats. This style, which did not last long, was at its height among the poor people just after the Exposition. It was a dull, hard felt, like a derby but as high as a "high hat" and shaped like a pyramid. A mighty large and imposing hat it was!

I had often stood before this shop and dreamed of a time when I could dress "elegantly." The day that Boucot had taken me to visit the publishers I had admired his Girondin even more than his overcoat with a velvet collar.

48

Now, I reasoned, in order to put up a good front as an artist, I must improve my appearance. I had to look "rich." So I hurried to a large clothing store on the Rue Ménilmontant called "The Economy."

The Louque and I chose a superb overcoat with a velvet collar like Boucot's. The material was of poor quality and it cost nine francs. And to go with the coat I selected a handsome Girondin of the three-franc class. You remember I had a very large head on a short dumpy body. So the crown of the Girondin had to be extra high because of my large headsize.

I looked like a dwarf wearing a giant's hat. Before the mirror, I saw that the result was not perfect, but, because I resembled the elegant Boucot, I thought I would become used to it.

I decided not to "dress up" until the day of my debut at Tourelles and then planned to put on my overcoat and my Girondin for the Thursday afternoon rehearsal. I was sure that my elegance would impress the Rue Julien Lacroix.

A real hat! A Girondin! Think of it! This was something! Before that I'd worn nothing but caps. I waited for Thursday like a young bride anxious to don her white dress.

Thursday arrived. I worked all morning, brushing my overcoat and waxing my shoes until I had blisters. And I tried on the Girondin at all angles. First I'd raise it in salute, then put it back a little to one side, and finally pose it nonchalantly on the back of my head. Though Mamma laughed at my airs, she admitted that I looked like a child of the rich.

After lunch I dressed and stole a last glance in the mirror. Then, casting a triumphant look at the Louque I set out. As I passed the concierge I bowed "Bon Jour." She was too stunned to answer.

My first hundred yards brought a strange silence to the Rue Julien Lacroix. Everyone stopped talking.

Going through the Ronce Arcade, one of the most dangerous spots of the district, I heard them saying, "Oh— oh—look at the clown—oh!"

That didn't sound good! I began to wonder if I could by any wild chance be ridiculous. Or were they jealous of my elegance? I could sense that it was my Girondin that was causing this stir. It was the enormous hat on top of my enormous head and my little short body.

But I couldn't turn back now. I straightened up and continued down the Rue Julien Lacroix. Then I started down the Rue de Belleville, which was even more crowded. I heard several more derogatory remarks about my Girondin. Then I arrived at Tourelles.

Caron, the comedian, asked me when I intended to put on my tails and my stovepipe. The artistes teased me kindly about my elegance.

I returned to the Rue Julien Lacroix by the same route. But by now I was getting pretty scared. The streets seemed ominously quiet. I rushed down Belleville so fast that sweat poured from under my Girondin onto my velvet collar.

People called after me,

"Long live the Mayor."

"Good day, doctor."

My fear turned to panic. Then I was running. Fifteen Rue Julien Lacroix was in sight and I had only two hundred yards more to go.

On a corner of Ronce Arcade I imagined I saw moving shadows. It was spooky. Then a long body emerged from the alley—two—three of them. They had been lying in wait for my return.

Before I could cry out for help I received such a blow on the top of my Girondin that the diabolical hat came down over my chin. Through the felt I could hear the chuckling of those blackguards.

Without even trying to adjust my hat I ran, like a headless man, straight toward number 15. I stumbled and fell. Someone picked me up and managed to draw me out from under my Girondin. Trembling I threw myself into the arms of the Louque, sobbing bitterly with humiliation.

I had thought myself so well dressed! Now I did not dare to put on a hat again until I was eighteen years old. In fact I have preferred caps ever since.

But even all this didn't stop me from becoming an entertainer!

8. I Begin to Live

ONLY THE MILITARY and the laboring classes can fully appreciate the luxury of sleeping late on winter mornings. Only those whose whole lives revolve around getting to work at seven in the morning know the painful sensation of leaping out of bed at dawn, still drowsy, to plunge under an icy tap for a brutal awakening.

During the time that I tried so many trades Paul and I arose together courageously. And then, after washing in cold water, we enjoyed the good coffee prepared by the Louque. After that we set out together for our workshops.

So a great advantage of my new singing job was that I could stay late in bed. As I watched Paul set out in the icy fog that first morning, I felt a little sad at the difference there would be in our two lives from now on. But I was not too sad to turn toward the wall for a good two hours of sleep while Mamma attended to her housework. Then I had the unutterable joy of coffee in bed. Ollé! How wonderful it was to be in show business. That coffee went to my head like brandy!

When I told my news to Boucot, he didn't seem sufficiently impressed. But at least he admitted that we could see more of each other now that I was my own master during the day.

Our trips to Paris became more frequent. Sometimes I would "go down" alone in my overcoat with the velvet collar and a fine new cap.

All the publishers knew me now as I was constantly looking for new songs. Some of them took a real interest in my career. Day by day I made new acquaintances among the stars of both sexes. The more important ones helped me because of my youth and my small size. The lesser known and the unknown were clearly jealous and implied that it would be better for me to continue my schooling than to try to compete with them.

I was a little over thirteen now and completely on my own. For in spite of Gilbert's interest in me he could do nothing when after three weeks the director decided to change his bill. He assured me that he liked me and would take me on again—later.

I had not expected to find myself on the street so suddenly. Now I asked Boucot if he would speak to Verner, the director of the Concert de Commerce, about me. He did and Verner sent for me. I arrived full of hope.

"You can sing between Boucot's two numbers," said Verner, "but as you are an extra on the program and can only do two songs I can't pay you what you have been getting at Tourelles. Absolutely impossible! I would be out of pocket. But if you'll take five francs for four days a week we can make a deal."

My throat tightened. How could this smiling director ask me to take a two-thirds cut? I tried to explain to him that, having left the workshop, I must take home at least nine francs a week to Mamma.

But he was inflexible, and right then and there I began to understand that a smile often hides a cold heart.

I told Mamma the bad news. To my astonishment she advised me not to give up so quickly but to try it out for several weeks. Then, if things didn't pick up, she said, I could always go back to the tack factory.

The next day I went down into Paris to try the small music halls. I stopped at La Ville Japonaise, a café on the Boulevard Strasbourg, and timidly asked for the owner.

"Good morning, M-m-madame," I stuttered, "I'm a singer looking for a p-public audition." She seemed amused and asked me to come back at eight o'clock. I galloped back to the Rue Julien Lacroix to prepare my props and practice my songs. I was too excited to eat.

At eight o'clock I was crammed into the corner of the dressing room that served for both men and women. The sight of a half-nude brunette putting on her stockings fascinated me. I dressed, made up, and went on, followed by the vision of the seated brunette. I sang without seeing or hearing anything. I didn't dare speak to the manager. Instead I spent the rest of the evening in the corner of the dressing room devouring the brunette with my eyes.

Finally the manager remembered me and asked the owner for her decision. My legs went weak with excitement when she said, "If you want to start Friday at eight

Chevalier showing Rivollet, author of *De Ménilmontant au Casino de Paris*, the place in the gate of the church of Ménilmontant where he crushed a finger as a boy.

Chevalier, at thirteen, posed for this picture postcard.

Chevalier at fourteen when he was just starting out as an entertainer.

Chevalier in his tramp costume at fifteen.

we will try you for a week. We can only give you three francs a day for two matinees and two evenings a week.

That was all I wanted to know! I signed the paper and returned on the double to wake up Paul and the Louque and announce that their "artist" would now bring in twenty francs a week! All records were broken!

That night I dreamed of the brunette. Perhaps it is a bit shocking that a child of thirteen should have had such carnal thoughts, but you must realize the position of a defenseless boy suddenly thrown into this sort of life. The Louque hardly knew how to read and write and had never known anything but housework and lace making. The dangers of show business were unknown to her. And Paul was unbelievably pure. I was rather like a puppy suddenly abandoned on the Boulevards.

I had no real friends and had to make my way in this murky world by instinct alone. I was ready to take in everything—the worst with the best. My poetic love for Georgette and my passion for Daudibert were forgotten now in my obsession for this well-rounded brunette.

The audience at La Ville Japonaise was made up mostly of old roués and their young mistresses. The combinations constantly changed.

A certain blonde seen one evening with a certain black beard would be found having her *eau de vie* the following night with an elderly character sporting a white moustache. These vicious old men and their tarts formed the core of the clientele. The rest were transients. You see, the Boulevard Strasbourg was a busy street and many traveling salesmen would stop for an hour at La Ville Japonaise while waiting for a train at Gare de l'Est.

This was an indifferent sort of audience. Often a whole act went by unapplauded. The old goats seemed more interested in their personal affairs.

Everyone from the director to the waiters had the stamp of this atmosphere. And if a performer had happened to have enough talent to be noisily applauded, I guess he'd have been fired for disturbing the quiet of this half café, half bawdy house.

My debut did not disturb *anyone*. The old men looked at me with jaundiced eye. The young women weren't interested at all. I was too young. In a word, everyone was satisfied.

Strasbourg Boulevard was really the center of café life. Opposite La Ville Japonaise were the Eldorado and the Scala, the top cafés. Scattered around this district were all of the low-grade publishers and song agents, all of the spangled costume merchants and the many little tradesmen whose only raison d'être was the multitude of singers. We felt that this district belonged to us little artists.

However, some of the clients of the little bars and cafés invaded our territory without our permission. There were several generations of ruffians whose only work consisted of playing cards—*bellotte, manille, jacquet*—while their women peddled their charms at a distance. These women never approached us entertainers. They understood that we did not fool on the job.

During my stay at La Ville Japonaise I learned that in this kind of life I had nothing to gain by being too honest and sincere. Each day as I left the matinee I passed a young brunette seated with the same old character at the back of the room. She smiled at me openly.

"You sang very well today, Monsieur Little Chevalier."

"It was very good. Bravo!" the man would say.

Timidly I would thank them, and one day they invited me to have a drink. Her beauty was on the vulgar side but she was undeniably attractive. The man didn't resent her pleasant manner to me. I was too small to be dangerous.

One day, however, as I was leaving I noticed that she was alone at the table. She stood up to speak and left the café with me.

"My friend has gone away for the day and I feel deserted," she said. "Would you mind if I dine at your restaurant with you? Oh, don't be afraid. I know you aren't rich and I'm inviting you."

Never before had I found myself in a situation like this. My first thought was that I would be able to take home thirty sous more than usual to Mamma. So I gladly accepted.

Familiarly she took my arm and, although I was a head shorter than she, my pride made me feel taller. She was very gay and kept drawing me closer and closer. I began to feel the same excitement that I had felt about the brunette in the dressing room. I sensed that I was setting out on an adventure over which I had no control.

We stopped at a bar and she insisted that we drink together like two pals. I blessed this new life where such things could happen all of a sudden.

After a better dinner than I was accustomed to we started back to the Boulevard by way of the Rue des Petites Ecuries. The Rue des Petites Ecuries was dimly lighted and there were many little corners and doorways along it.

"Ah!" she exclaimed suddenly, "You are so cute—I just have to kiss you!" The first time she kissed me on the cheek, like a sister. At the next doorway she gave me a long kiss on the mouth. No one had ever kissed me like that and I didn't like it. I felt stifled. Then I wanted to wipe off my mouth and spit. But after about ten doorways I grew to like this game and began to return her kisses. As we parted she promised that we would repeat our escapade on our next "free" day.

That evening the indifference of the audience at La Ville Japonaise was matched by my own. I did my work adequately but my mind was on this new unknown world of sex.

I did not speak of this at home. Inside I felt that it was all wrong. Already I was fighting the great battle between prudence and carnal instinct.

The next day my girl friend was not at the matinee; but as I left, her old man called out to me:

"Eh! Young man!"

As I approached him there was an atmosphere of menace. What could I do? I was so inexperienced at this sort of thing.

The old man spoke first of himself. He listed all of his generosities and he described his deep feelings for the lady. He knew that we had dined together and he was a little jealous. He said he was sure there had been nothing between us—I was so young and had such an honest face. But he begged me to have pity on him and tell him the truth. He felt he did not deserve to be humiliated.

"Tell me exactly what happened," he begged. "I promise to say nothing to her. I must know! I am so unhappy."

I didn't realize the incongruity of this scene between a boy of thirteen and an old man of seventy. And the more he talked the more I could see that it was up to me to be honest with this poor generous man who suffered so.

"Monsieur," I said, "since you appeal to my honesty, I think it's my duty to tell you that this young woman does not return your love. She is not worthy of it, Monsieur, or of your sorrow."

And in a burst of sincerity I told him every detail of our walk from the restaurant and even of the pleasure that I had felt. In my innocence I hoped to cure him of his fatal passion. Poor man! I felt so sorry for him that I could have wept on his shoulder.

' He listened to the whole thing. Then looking at me coldly he said, "Good-bye, young man."

I left with the complacent feeling that I had acted as an honest fellow. The next afternoon I had not taken six steps on the Boulevard de Strasbourg when my pretty brunette appeared. Her face was transformed with fury.

"You little skunk!" she screamed.

I didn't know what stand to take. I was more surprised than insulted.

"Well, you little skunk—what's the matter with you? I'm not a bar maid you know—what manners!"

She raised her arm and started toward me—

"Little skunk!" she bellowed, "My friend has chucked me because of your nastiness. I'll break your neck!"

I turned and ran like the devil through the crowd that had gathered.

The next afternoon I appeared at La Ville Japonaise half scared to death. I didn't dare look at anyone. I even trembled as I sang.

Then I saw them. They were sitting arm in arm in their usual place at the back. I waited as long as possible but finally I had to leave. As I drew near their table she saw me. She kissed the old man lovingly. Then as I passed by they murmured together softly:

"Little skunk!"

9. Experiences

WHEN MY ENGAGEMENT at the Ville Japonaise ended I was given a public audition at the Casino de Montmartre on the Boulevard de Clichy and was taken on at the same salary. I could still take home twenty-one francs a week.

Montmartre was the hangout of most of the pimps and tough guys of Paris and the Casino was their favorite afternoon rendezvous. It was very popular with all the queer fish and loafers. To pass the time while their women "worked," they preferred entertainment to card playing. You can imagine that it was not a very charming audience.

There for the first time I saw entertainers really slaughtered by an audience. Many of us left the room in tears. These hecklers were not unusually cruel to the regular performers, but they enjoyed hurling insults at the poor devils who auditioned here every day. In fact these charming fellows considered the auditions the high spot of the afternoon.

The manager knew how to please his clientele and he let anyone try out who wanted to. The more ridiculous the performer, the heartier the laughter.

Perhaps because of my youth the audience was not too hard on me. This was my first experience with real beasts, and the fact that they did not devour me gave me more self-confidence for the future.

After two weeks at the Casino and a short run at La Fourmi on the Boulevard Barbès I decided to get an agent. I went to see Dalos, who had once been an entertainer himself. Old artists often become agents just as old boxers become managers. He occupied two little rooms in an old building in the Passage Brady. One was a reception room without chairs and the other an office without a desk. Every Monday the directors of the small Paris café concerts came there to fill out their programs for the week. Hungry show people crowded the little room and overflowed onto the stairway. From time to time Dalos would pop out of his office and choose one of the anxious applicants. Then, as the rest watched the door like beggers, the lucky guy would come out a little later proudly waving a contract.

Dalos noticed me right away because I was the only child in the room. He was amazed when I showed him my references and he took my name and address.

When I went back the next day he had an engagement for me at the Concert de l'Univers, Avenue de Wagram. Would I accept five francs an evening with a Sunday matinee?

Would I accept it? I ask you! My record was broken again!

Old Hamel was the director of the Concert de l'Univers. He was a bulldog type with a quick temper, but underneath he wasn't a bad guy at all. He wandered constantly among the tables while the show was on and made a habit of speaking to the performers from wherever he happened to be.

"Very good!" he would call out. "Bravo, my boy!" Or, sometimes he warned, "If you keep on singing that trash I'll have to kick you out!"

The audience at the Concert de l'Univers was made up mostly of middle-class people and servants. They were easy to please and welcomed me with a warmth I had never known before.

From watching Boricot, Serjius, and Dorville I had developed a comic style that imitated first one and then another of them. And to cap the climax I always added a pinch of Dranem.

That first night I gave one of Claudius' monologues:

> *Iron willed,*
> *I only know*
> *When one is a man*
> *It must show!*

I illustrated this by putting my hands in my pockets and making a vulgar gesture. That made the customers rock with laughter.

Because of my small size and my childish face, the more obscene my gestures became, the more the audience applauded.

They kept me for three months at the Concert de l'Univers. For twelve weeks I traveled back and forth on the metro. I had to learn six new songs every week. My "public" became more and more interested in me as I quickly caught on to their taste. With no one to advise me and no sound judgment of my own to depend upon, I came to rely more and more on dirty songs and jokes.

Like all the cabarets, the Concert de l'Univers had its "Mayol." The chambermaids and cooks sighed over Erard, a huge giant of a man with effeminate airs. They kept calling him back until he had sung all of Mayol's hits from "Tout au Clou" (Everything's Up the Spout) to "Viens Poupoule" (Come Darling).

He always brought his wife, a little trick from Avignon whom he had married before his rise in the capital. She was very proud of him and he was graciousy condescending to her as she cared for his costumes and even prompted him in his songs.

Erard was clumsy and ponderous by nature, but constantly now he cultivated the airs of a temperamental female star.

One evening, however, he forgot his pose for a moment. His wife, who was horribly jealous, found a love letter in his pocket while he was out front singing. Soon after he returned to the dressing room we heard through the thin partition the start of a noisy argument. At first, in a surprised and injured tone, he denied everything. He was proving that even when provoked he could keep his dignity and elegance. But these tactics got him nowhere with his wife. Instead she really let herself go now and showered our refined friend with all kinds of abuse.

He endured this flow of words for several minutes in silence. Then our dainty singer became his true self. The walls began to shake with such a tirade of obscene language as we had never heard. There followed a dull thud, and judging by Madame Erard's screams she was through talking for that night.

Then after a few moments of silence the door opened and she came out with a black eye, leaning submissively on the arm of her conqueror.

With his white silk scarf around his neck, his hat on the front of his head, and his silver-headed cane, M. Erard was "Mayol" once again. Swaying his hips he murmured politely as he passed us, "You see, dear friends, even if one is well brought up and distinguished, sometimes women give one such a pain in the - - - that one must discipline them."

So saying he waved to us coquettishly and slunk out like a large and weary prima donna.

Our comedian came from Morocco and was named Pedro Vivès. I thought him the most charming man of the troupe. He was good looking and kind and gentle. But I found out that he was too polite to be honest.

One evening a friend of his came to call for him. He was very elegant, with beautiful rings and a little blond mustache. I noticed that his face was powdered.

65

The two of them invited me to have a drink before going home. I said I had to catch the metro, but the pretty man promised that he himself would take me home in a cab.

Now I had not been in a cab since Mamma had rushed me to the hospital with a broken finger. So, being naïve, I saw no reason to turn down a nice ride with this amiable fellow.

We had our drink at a café in the Avenue de Wagram. After saying good night to Pedro Vivés I found myself seated beside my new friend in a closed cab. I said something about his perfume and he replied that he loved perfume, silk underwear, and all beautiful things. Then he took my hand and stroking it he gave me a long strange look that I did not understand. As we talked his arm slipped around my neck.

Suddenly I was frightened. Here was an unknown danger. Then he tried to kiss me! I fought him off like a demon and this nauseating battle lasted for some time. Finally we arrived at my home and I felt obliged to thank him for the taxi ride.

As I went upstairs I realized that what had happened was too serious to tell Paul and the Louque. They might make me give up a profession where such extraordinary things could happen. I was ashamed and disgusted without knowing exactly why.

The next day at the cabaret I told Pedro Vivès all about it, right in front of all the other performers. I said the man must be crazy and asked Pedro what he thought about it.

The comedian turned pale and explained to our angry friends that he considered me old enough to defend myself if I didn't like that kind of thing.

So now I knew something else. Not only must I beware of attached women but also I must avoid certain mustachioed ones.

They'd never catch me again in a cab ride with a powdered "man."

10. *A Real Little Man*

AFTER A LONG STAND at the Concert de l'Univers I began a tour of small cafés and *bouis-bouis* of the Capital. Sometimes through my agent Dalos and sometimes by applying in person I got to sing at the Café Persan, the Bateaux Parisiens, the Café de la Presse, and many others.

Dalos got me my first contracts in the provinces. I started out at the Folies-Bergère at Havre where I got thirty-five francs for three days, plus traveling expenses. There for the first time I saw the ocean.

Everything went well until I hit Tours, where I had a

very painful adventure. My stay in this place had started out well. The atmosphere of the town was congenial, my director was satisfied, and everything seemed swell. I was doing exactly what I wanted to do. I was helping out at home, and I was enjoying a certain amount of independence. A perfect setup!

Then one evening after the show a traveling salesman invited me to lunch with him the following day at a restaurant outside Tours. He too was alone in the town and I found him a very congenial chap. It seemed like a good idea.

The next morning I sharpened my appetite with a brisk walk of several miles. Then I joined my generous traveling salesman for an *apéritif* at the main café of the town.

We were having a good time and he insisted that we follow our first drink with two more. I was gasping after the second, and the third went right to my head. Finally we staggered out of the café laughing noisily.

I had never felt like this before but I liked the sensation. Then we washed down an excellent lunch with some good wine and life seemed pretty wonderful. What a fine fellow this guy was!

After lunch we went to a *brasserie* for a cordial. I had never drunk hard liquor straight before and this seemed like a good time to begin.

My host ordered two rums. At first it burned my throat and made me cough. But soon a warm feeling of well-being enveloped me. How delightful everything was!

The second rum went down more easily. The voices of the other customers were beginning to ring strangely in my ears, but I didn't mind that at all.

Hup! Down went a third rum!

All this time we were seated, so I had no warning of the dangers in store for me. And I suppose that the traveling salesman thought the whole thing a great joke.

I ordered two more rums. By now every time I said anything my voice sounded so funny to me that I laughed and laughed.

We gulped down rum after rum—8, 9, 10 glasses followed each other in quick succession. I seemed to be in another world—a nice, carefree world.

When we finally noticed that I was late for the Alcazar I stood up for the first time since lunch. Oh! How everything whirled! It was extraordinary! I had to sit down again. My drinking partner almost died laughing.

But *I* wasn't laughing any more. I knew I had to get to my dressing room in time for the show.

I stuttered a boozy "thank you" and "good-bye." Then with a desperate effort I stood up and staggered to the door. I managed the short distance to the Alcazar by holding onto the walls.

I saw the passers-by through a fog—they looked at me in surprise and amusement and seemed to be saying something. I could see their eyes and their moving lips, but I couldn't hear anything at all.

I dragged myself to the dressing room, soaked with

sweat. That pale face in the mirror didn't seem to belong to me. I began to undress. A friend asked if I was sick but I couldn't answer him. There was a whirlwind and a ringing of bells, and then my head left my body. Mon Dieu!

They picked me up dead drunk and carried me to my rooming house. A kind singer put me to bed with compresses on my poor head. There was no question of doing my work.

"This young Chevalier is making a good start. What a little guttersnipe!" That's what my colleagues thought of me.

When I woke up the next day sick at heart and with a terrible head, I rushed to the Alcazar to make my apologies. The manager was raging mad.

"Never set foot in this building again," he shouted. "Your behavior is scandalous. There's no excuse for it. Go to the cashier and get your money for the four days you've been here. Then get out. You're fired!"

Frantically I pled with him, "Monsieur, I swear I didn't know that alcohol could do this to me. It's the first time I've ever been drunk. Monsieur, I beg of you, don't let me go! I must take home some money."

But he was pitiless. He even threatened to send for the police. He kept right on insulting me until I finally left.

Out of my skimpy earnings I could pay for my room at the boarding house and buy my return ticket, but I would not have anything left over to take back to my mother. I was in tears. Then an understanding singer at my pension suggested that I hand my bag to him through the window of my room and cut out for my train without paying the landlady. It was as easy as that! He assured me that this was an old trick in show business. And after all, he said, I could always send on the money with my apologies when things improved. This made his scheme sound better, and we carried out the plan to the letter.

The train for Paris didn't leave for a half hour after I boarded it, and those thirty minutes were a nightmare. With my third-class ticket in hand I hid under the seat. I had visions of the whole town up in arms with the proprietor shouting, "Stop thief!" and the police running to the station.

Finally I heard the whistle of the locomotive. The train started and I came out of my hiding place. For a long time I sobbed with shame and self disgust.

At home I told Mamma that the show had suddenly closed but that I'd been able to save a few francs for her.

Right away I went into a frenzy of work trying to forget this whole deplorable adventure. The director at Tours had written to Dalos complaining about me, so I didn't dare go to him for a job.

Luckily I was asked to return to the Casino de Montmartre at five francs a day. Then I was raised to seven at the Concert de l'Univers. Things were going well again and the Chevaliers were able to move from the Rue Julien Lacroix into a little two-room apartment on the court at 15 Faubourg du Temple, near the Place de la République.

Everything went fine until Paul met and fell in love with a young Belleville girl. Then he told Mamma he wanted to marry her.

It was the same old story. The disease seemed to run in the family! Mamma and I begged him to wait until I was a little older but that idea didn't get us anywhere. He was in love, he said, and had his own life to live. He promised us a little out of his salary every week.

Mamma, Paul, and I cried a long time over this sad parting. And then the Louque and I found ourselves alone.

I was now her sole support. At fourteen and a half I was the head of the family!

For several days Mamma and I felt lost without Paul, but soon I began to enjoy having her all to myself. We became closer than ever, and during meals I told her all about my job and my friends. I sang my new songs and asked her opinion of them. I adored her, and her dependence on me filled me with a real sense of responsibility.

Since I had been steadily employed for several months now, I gave the Louque my whole salary and she allowed me a few francs each week for pin money.

But I didn't like the location of our new apartment in the Faubourg du Temple. At number 15 we were half way between the Boulevard de Belleville and the Place de la République. It was neither in the suburbs nor in the center of Paris. Now I found an apartment at 118 Faubourg Saint Martin, almost at the corner of the Boulevard

Magenta. It consisted of two rooms on the sixth floor on the court. This put us right in the center of the music world and I was well pleased with the neighborhood.

After a long stand at the Concert de l'Univers I got my first engagement on the Boulevards at the Petit Casino on the Boulevard Montmartre. There we had matinees and evening performances every day.

The Petit Casino was considered the main springboard for music hall success at that time. Because of its location there was a steady stream of people coming and going there at all hours. The audience was a pretty rough crowd and it was hard to win their attention. But playing there was a good test of ability. And since this was where most of the important singers had made their start, I was all keyed up to make good. But my first song at the Petit Casino was greeted with unfriendly silence. Oh yes, at the end there was a little scattered applause, but on the whole my effort to please met with indifference. But up to now I had always made a hit with my monologue, so I launched into

> *Will of iron,*
> *That I know,*
> *When one is a man*
> *It must show.*

Desperately trying to get a laugh, I exaggerated even more than usual the vulgar gesture that went with these words. However, to my anguished surprise there wasn't a smile in

73

the room. There was only a sort of murmur as I left the floor.

My third song, a great success at the Concert de l'Univers, was called "Look at Monsieur Trottin." In this I represented a young delivery boy on his way to deliver a carton containing a woman's chemise and pants and corset. During the first chorus I opened the box and put on the chemise over my costume. At the second chorus I put the corset around me. The belly laugh was supposed to come at the third chorus when I put on the drawers, with the chemise sticking out through the large holes in front and behind.

This effect had never failed anywhere. It was sure fire.

But not this day—not at the Petit Casino!

Just as I started the second chorus, I heard a strong voice shout, "Enough! That's disgusting. Send that boy back to school!"

Everyone in the room must have agreed, since no one came to my rescue. On the contrary, as the hubbub grew I could hear them saying, "The nerve of that child is absolutely disgraceful! They shouldn't allow such a scandalous exhibition."

I couldn't believe my ears. But finally I realized my disgrace and, hanging my head, I left the room.

The manager, a retired imitator of Paulus, just laughed and said, "This happened to Paulus—it can happen just as well to you."

But my heart was broken and I went to my dressing

room and cried steadily for over an hour, completely discouraged. My small amount of self-confidence had evaporated in a fear of the future.

After the matinee I went to meet Paul at his workshop
and told him the whole sad story. I was scared to go back
that evening, in fact I was trembling with fright at the
thought of it. But Paul comforted me the best he could and
finally we decided that I must face the music.

That evening I sang so sedately that I would have been
O.K. at a church bazaar. This time there was no applause
but at least they didn't put me out. In fact, during that
whole week at the Petit Casino I had this same kind of
icy reception. I was unhappy and had lost faith in myself. Why had no one warned me that my songs and monologues might shock certain kinds of audiences?

Apparently I would have to learn everything by sad
experience. I was heavy hearted and ashamed and felt sure
that everyone in the Faubourg Saint Martin knew of my
failure.

Now the summer season began and engagements became scarcer. I was out of work for weeks at a time. The
Louque and I lived in poverty that whole summer. We
ate nothing but baked potatoes and washed them down with
a *tisane* made from cherry stems. I couldn't even get the
holes repaired in the soles of my shoes. I had to line them
with folded newspaper. Paul helped us a little but he had
his own expenses to meet and couldn't spare much. God

75

knows I tried, but all my attempts to find work met with failure.

Some Sundays I was able to pick up a few francs at the little cafés on the Seine. But I was horribly discouraged about not being able to take proper care of the Louque and almost regretted that I had given up my chances of learning a trade.

One Sunday I was reduced to singing in a café at Gargan for three francs plus the collection. After every act the entertainers passed a saucer and were allowed to keep what they collected.

I had never taken up a collection and I was ashamed to do so now. After each act I passed the saucer with a trembling hand and I would hardly wait to see if the customer was reaching for his pocket or not. Naturally this technique produced a pitifully small number of sous.

Now, besides myself, a robust Breton bard with a very loud voice was the only male member of the troupe. He got a lot more applause and many more sous when he passed the saucer. After each performance he came back and proudly showed me his overflowing collection. I was more sad than envious, but he had no pity for me and just chuckled with self-satisfaction.

After this had happened several times I decided to watch and see for myself how my colleague managed to do it. I found that he became very humble as he held out the saucer. He didn't just pass it—he actually begged. Then just before he joined me I saw him put his hand in his own pocket and add some change from his other collections.

It was disgusting to see a man of his age stoop to such low tricks just to discourage a poor struggling boy. For a moment I almost felt like giving up a profession where such things could happen.

But learning a new trade would mean starting all over again at an apprentice's salary, and the Louque and I could hardly live on that. However, I looked at the want ads in the paper and found an offer—three francs a day "for anyone possessing penmanship fine enough to address letters." The applicant was supposed to answer by letter so that they could judge his qualifications. Carefully I made several sample letters and sent them off with high hopes.

The Louque and I anxiously watched for the mailman each morning with beating hearts. But two, three, five, then ten days went by and nothing arrived. Our poverty turned to despair. Now I was ready to accept any kind of work and I expected the worst.

Then one morning I received an envelope addressed to me with the letterhead of the "Parisiana" Music Hall. Overcome with excitement I opened it. It was an invitation to see the management the following day at two o'clock. An angel from heaven could not have brought us greater happiness.

Thinking that perhaps this would be the end of our misery, the Louque and I hugged each other as we laughed and cried for joy.

The next day I set out in my shabby but clean clothes and my shoes with the leaky soles. Parisiana, the greatest music hall of the Boulevards, had just been bought by Paul Ruez who formerly had directed La Fourmi on the Boulevard Barbès. Apparently he had stumbled across my name on an old program while looking for artists for his autumn revue.

Well, to make a long story short, I left his office with a contract for the duration of his revue, *Satyre Bouchonne*. I was to sing at the opening of the show, then fill in or understudy several small roles. Wanting to make the most of this good luck, I boldly asked for ten francs a day. Actually I would have taken half of that. But they offered me nine and the contract was signed then and there.

Usually a revue of this importance lasted a minimum of six months. I could count, therefore, on nine francs a day for that length of time.

How happy the Louque and I were that evening! Our potatoes seemed like a great delicacy and the *tisane* went to our heads like wine. We made plans: we decided to put aside half of my salary each day. We must never again experience the terrible torture we had just been through.

Mamma could manage our household very well on twenty-one francs a week. I would have a franc and a half a day for pocket money. And best of all, four francs and a half were to be entered each day in the beautiful new savings bank book.

Six months at nine francs a day! That was a fortune!

If an impresario had come along then and offered me a contract for life at ten francs a day I would have kissed his hands and signed it with joy!

11. *Parisiana*

IT WAS AUGUST, 1904, and the Paris season was getting under way. Mon Dieu! but the city seemed happy to be alive! Each evening a bunch of us young fellows strolled down the Boulevards to the Madeleine. Then we cut across the Rue Royale to the Champs Elysées and finally collapsed under the huge trees surrounding the Ambassadeurs.

As we went along the Boulevards we tried to act very Bohemian. We saluted the pretty women riding in open carriages or strolling about with their lovers or husbands. As we passed the crowded sidewalke cafés single file, we sometimes showed off our eccentric dance steps.

In spite of my bravado I had to stop every once in a while to rearrange the folded newspaper that covered the hole in my shoe. However, I would soon be able to remedy this with my pay from the Parisiana. We were putting on a show there now at the same time that we were rehearsing for the big revue.

Once in a while we were lucky enough to be hired for the claque at the Ambassadeurs. A row at the back of the room was reserved for this institution. The claque was chosen from the first arrivals who couldn't afford the price of admission. But if we spent too much time on the boulevards we had to be contented with listening outdoors under the trees. We were like starving kitchen boys at the Ritz smelling the aromas from the chef's dishes.

Mayol was performing at the Ambassadeurs that summer. But sometimes, before the great man came on, we went near by to l'Alcazar d'Eté to hear Polin and Dranem.

We usually felt a little sad as we returned homeward. The great artists we had seen were so wonderful. Unconsciously we compared ourselves with them and felt sure that we could never attain such heights.

At the beginning of September the walls of Paris were covered with Capiello's huge posters announcing the opening of "Parisiana" starring Vilbert, the gay tenor from the Midi.

But the opening failed to make much of a stir. The Parisian gentry were not all back from the country yet and everyone knew that this show was just a preliminary to the real season. The big event would be the opening of the revue, *Satyre Bouchonne*.

We rehearsed for this every day for about a month. Besides being an understudy, I was in the back row of the chorus. I was at least a head shorter than the others and often heard Verdellet, the author of the revue, complain that I destroyed the harmony of the setting. So I stood on tiptoe as much as possible.

One day I was trying a little too hard to do well and Verdellet noticed me.

"Well, Chevalier," he howled, "you're just about the clumsiest person I've ever seen on the stage. You'd do better as a chimney sweep. Better artists than you are dying of hunger."

Terrified, I went through the scene again like an automaton. I was sure that Verdellet was going to fire me, but luckily he soon forgot all about me again.

The opening night was a brilliant affair. Well ahead of time I stood on the sidewalk opposite The Parisiana, watching the bustle. There was a long line for the unreserved seats. Then came the carriages with the people for the orchestra seats. The most important people arrived in expensive automobiles. There were Dietrichs and Mars' and Panhard Levassors which were supposed to go thirty miles an hour. To me it all seemed like something out of the *Thousand and One Nights*.

Later, through a hole in the curtain, Carjol, the comedian, pointed out all the celebrities. He showed me Léopold, the King of Belgium, with his long beard, and Cléo Mérode, the Madonna-like dancer. Catulle Mendès, the

81

most important critic of the day, was there with Le Bargy who wore a black straw hat for the occasion.

"There's Mistinguett," said Carjol. She's just sung at the Eldorado and has come here to be seen. Those sad eyes of hers and that childlike smile make her the most exciting woman here tonight. Have you seen her on the stage? She's really hot stuff! And there's Liane de Pougy —she is not for the likes of us. And Jeanne Lorrain, with her huge rings and made up like a tart—she's not for us either, kid!"

So this was the high life of Paris! I was dazzled. What the devil did I have in common with these strange, charming creatures?

The show was a huge success. There was a constant shower of flowers and applause from the audience.

One of the favorites of the revue was the very attractive Lucy Jousset. She was a good comedienne and had a pretty voice. But she never looked at me once during the whole time we were at the Parisiana. I wondered why Vilbert, the star, got to go to her dressing room so often. He reappeared each time looking even more self-satisfied than usual. I didn't think he was so handsome as all that!

Max Dearly, the Don Juan of the moment, was also smitten with the charms of the fair Jousset and often came to see her too.

I felt as remote from all of these glamorous people as any stage-struck fan who stands at the stage entrance on a gala evening. Whenever possible I seated myself on the stairway leading to the stars' dressing rooms and, fascinated, watched the coming and going.

But I did draw a certain amount of attention to myself after all. As the show progressed I began to grow physically. You remember that when I first started at the Parisiana I had been a head shorter than anyone in the chorus. At the end of six months I was a head taller than the tallest. My fellow entertainers couldn't believe their eyes and thought it must be some trick. It was phenomenal!

Now that we had enough money, the Louque and I went to renew my wardrobe at the Carreau du Temple. This was a kind of gigantic flea market where all the shopkeepers of Paris could find merchandise displayed on tight-packed shelves. At the Carreau they carried everything from officers' uniforms to the most miserable second-hand rags; from judges' costumes to lace underwear. They even sold hernia belts.

I unearthed a wonderful costume. It was a sack suit with great wide shoulders, very much in the extreme American style. It must have belonged originally to a very fat character. They asked fifteen francs for this prize number, but after a good deal of heated bargaining I got it for twelve.

Mamma refitted it as best she could and then, certain that I cut a sporty and up-to-date figure, I hurried out to strut proudly on the Boulevard.

In those days I was very thin and gangly, and I must have looked like a broomstick lost in that huge suit. From the reaction of my friends I soon realized that I still had much to learn about elegance of dress.

When I arrived in this outfit at the Parisiana that evening, Fragson called out in his metallic voice before all the assembled company, "Tell us, Chevalier, is that your Grandfather's suit?"

Everyone laughed and I turned scarlet. Once more I had the feeling of shame that comes to me so easily. I had hoped that the manager would notice my new height and my splendid clothes and rehire me for the next season. But apparently I didn't make much of an impression on him, for my contract was not renewed.

Once more I was out of a job.

12. *I Get Around*

AT THE END of my engagement at the Parisiana I had five hundred francs in the savings bank and a completely new outfit of clothes. The Louque and I had kept to our resolution to save half my salary for a rainy day.

Once more I started the rounds of the agents. But now I called myself "Chevalier M" in the manner of several stars of the time. Then too I didn't want to be confused with the eccentric artist Louis Chevalier or the provincial comedian Emile Chevalier.

However, all this swank failed to get me any very good offers. And I had to take thirty-five francs for three days a week at the Eden-Concert in Asnières. It was sort of tough going back to a week-to-week existence.

Really I hadn't learned much at the Parisiana. In fact I left there with even less self-confidence than before. The sophisticated atmosphere had made me realize how simple and inexperienced I was. I left that music hall feeling a little like an extra servant in an impressive household, hired only to help out for a short time.

But now, thank God, the Eden Concert fitted me to a T. Here I performed for an audience of suburbanites, of bookmakers and unpretentious bourgeois, and they took to me right away. I sang Dranem's songs and added a Ménilmontant flavor that was my own. These people loved to exchange snappy banter with the performers, and I was getting pretty good at this kind of thing. And now I was big enough so that my slightly smutty jokes no longer surprised anyone.

It was nice to have an audience of my own again. The people of Asnières took me to their heart. As soon as I appeared in the room someone would shout, "Hello there, little Chevalier! How goes it?"

I became a part of the establishment and ended up by staying there the whole season. Those friendly people restored my self-confidence. And it was at Eden-Concert that I began to take on a personality of my own instead of just imitating other and superior artists.

Now I was offered a week at la Scala in Brussels at twenty francs a day. The Louque and I were so excited about this amazing raise that we celebrated in a fine restaurant for the first time in our lives. We had a good dinner at le Drouant. And I guess we were a trifle tipsy at the end of it.

The first thing next morning Mamma was down by the concierge's door. Every tenant as he passed by had to have a look at the phenomenal contract proving that her son would now earn twenty francs a day in Belgium.

There were polite "Ohs!" and "Ahs!" and they exclaimed, "How lucky you are, Madame Chevalier, to have such a son!"

Of course the proud Louque told then how she had made me keep on when I had been so disheartened the year before.

In Brussels the people were just as cordial as those in Asnières had been. My engagement there had lasted a month. I was in love with my public, my job, and that smiling, gracious town.

It is true that I then had to take a salary cut at the Palais d'Eté at Lille. But in this profession you must always stay active. When you aren't working you not only earn nothing but you spend more. So you are doubly in the soup.

CHEVALIER

Chevalier at sixteen in another tramp costume.

LA REVUE DE L'ALCAZAR
Chevalier *dans l'Hygiénique*
Moi j'suis hygiénique avant tout

Still a different tramp costume. Chevalier is seventeen.

The Louque—Chevalier's mother.

Chevalier, at twenty, with
his mother.

Fortunately Lille kept me for two months. Boy, this was something like it!

On my return to Paris I had two thousand francs of savings and had acquired quite a reputation on the Boulevard de Strasbourg. I was now sixteen.

13. Marseilles

WHEN THE MANAGER of the Alcazar at Marseilles came to Paris to make his bookings for the winter show he sent for me. I left his hotel with contracts for a three-months tour to sing at Marseilles, Nice, Lyons, Bordeaux, Avignon, and several other southern towns. This was like riding on a magic carpet!

Once more I wanted a new wardrobe to match the occasion. In the music halls I had once worked with some English acrobats and had greatly admired the thick checked jackets that they wore in town. In the Rue Geoffroy Marie there was a store advertising "Remnants from the great tailors." They had a big choice of English clothing. I unearthed a good loud suit nearly my size, but it was drab beside the overcoat that I chose. This garment had the most aggressive green checks that any Scot ever

87

dreamed up—decidedly a flamboyant item. I was crazy about it. Now I could go on my trip dressed like a rich Englishman.

I completed my costume with an oversized cap from London and a pair of thick-soled boots. I was a sensation on the Boulevard de Strasbourg! Those heavy Scots woolens and sturdy leather shoes filled me with a sense of well-being. This made up for those months of patching my soles with newspaper. I am afraid that I will always have to fight my taste for the too loud and the too solid, implanted in me by years of poverty.

Finally the big day came and the train pulled into the Marseilles station at ten o'clock in the morning. With a bag in each hand I started for the Alcazar, which was on the other side of town. On the way I kept seeing huge posters advertising the evening performance. Dalbret led the list of names of the troupe. But I found my name, along about the middle, in large letters too. Seeing it there I almost fell over backward.

I stopped in my tracks. Everything that I had ever heard about Marseilles was spinning through my mind. My thoughts went something like this:

"This is Marseilles—Marseilles, do you understand? This is the famous theater where gangs shoot at each other across the balconies. This audience never stints its praise or its dislike. In Marseilles they tear off your ears with your earrings or cut off your finger with your rings to get the job done more quickly. At least you don't have to worry about jewelry, Maurice, my boy."

At the theater Franck, the manager, greeted me with, "Hello, young man, get ready. You'd better start rehearsing your number."

The stage was full of acrobats arranging their props, and scenery lifters were busily working on the backdrops. The orchestra was ready to help the performers rehearse.

Now it was up to me! Timidly I explained my little tricks to the orchestra leader. He started out. A hoarse croak came from my throat. The conductor looked up. What the hell was this?

Franck was obviously uneasy. Marius, who tended the gas lights (we didn't have electricity yet), shrugged his shoulders. Francois, the one-eyed stagehand, scratched his head. Things certainly didn't look so good for me.

"Shall I lower the key?" asked the leader, taking pity.

"No, no Monsieur," I assured him, "It'll be all right. You'll see. It's just the trip, you know—fatigue—but I'll be O.K. in front of the audience.

They all looked at each other as if to say, "Poor kid! They'll make mincemeat out of him tonight!"

After the rehearsal I took a long walk around the town alone. I was astounded to hear people talking in an accent different from that of Paris—and what an accent! And what a bustle and clatter there was on La Canebière, the Rue Saint-Ferréol, and the Allées de Meilhan.

Back at my little pension opposite the Gymnase Theatre

89

I couldn't swallow a bit of dinner. They tried to encourage me. As if I cared! I knew I was sunk. To begin with, I had no voice. Then I felt sure my Parisian accent would jar the customers.

That night the Alcazar was packed. There were rows and rows of heads, mostly in military caps.

The audience didn't pay much attention to the first act. There was a steady hubbub of conversation. Nothing went wrong in the second act until Bertho appeared. He was a veteran of the music halls, but he had stage fright that night. His voice was naturally very much like a goat's but now he bleated more than usual because he was scared. Then he began to do cartwheels in time to the music.

During his first two songs we had heard several threatening "bah bah's" from the balcony. But those cartwheels really did it.

A man in the front of the orchestra stood up and shouted "Bravo!"

Slowly turning toward the surprised audience, then back to Bertho, he repeated, "Bravo!"

Bertho stared at him round-eyed. The audience began to squirm.

Once more the man howled, "Bravo, what a dancer!" and sat down very pleased with himself.

After that the whole audience broke loose.

Bertho rushed from the stage and ran head first into a wall of the wing, mad and terrified at the same time.

Next a rather pretty woman named Morlaye came on

to sing songs from Montmartre. One of them satirized the Russo-Japanese war. Each refrain ended with:

Throw out General Oku.

(It seems there was a Japanese general of this name.)

The customers didn't go for the acid wit of Montmartre. And like all good Montmartre songs this one had many verses. The audience became more and more restless. For the fifth time the singer repeated:

Throw out General Oku.

As Morlaye started the sixth verse you could feel a tension in the crowd. She came once more to the last line of the chorus—with exactly the same rhythm and in just the same key. Suddenly a large strapping fellow rose up in the balcony and drowned her out with a great shout: "And you know what you can do with General Oku!"

This subtle witticism delivered in a Marseillais accent made a great hit. The audience gave the fellow a tremendous ovation and the poor woman left the stage in tears.

Right after this the orchestra attacked my introduction and I went on stage more dead than alive. The spectators kept right on laughing. They were rocking and slapping their thighs. I waited, not knowing what to do or say.

I just stood there for a while and finally the room calmed down and I began my first song.

My voice sounded muffled. I couldn't seem to make myself heard at all.

My verses were met with the silence of the morgue. Although my heart was heavy, I pretended not to notice and started a comic monologue.

Have you ever been in the position of a mediocre clown, grotesquely dressed and painted with rouge? You know you've damn well got to be funny—and you aren't funny at all. Well, that's what happened to me. As I went off the stage there was just a vague murmur. Out of the corner of my eye I saw Franck's stricken expression.

Desperately I began my "Rondeau Populaire." This was a medley of well-known songs.

Could I believe my ears? The audience had started to laugh—and it wasn't malicious laughter, either.

I was applauded loudly at the end and the danger was past—we were friends after all.

The fourth song went like a breeze:

> *There goes another pane of glass,*
> *And I see the glazier pass,*
>   *Chasseur, Chasseur.*
> *In your tail you have a pain,*
>   *Chasseur, Chasseur.*
> *Do you want the hand of sister*
> *To rub it for you Mister?*
> *There goes another pane of glass,*
> *Here comes the glazier past.*

I wore a toy Képi on my head. As I sang I marched around the stage blowing into a little gun and pretending it was a trumpet.

This byplay really won them over. As I passed the wing I heard Franck call out, "That's the way—you've really got them going now!"

When I finished, the applause was deafening. It had been a narrow escape but luckily I had hit the bull's eye.

I only dared risk one short fast encore, then I was back in my dressing room and my knees were shaking.

As in a dream I heard Franck say, "My boy, you've captured the provinces!"

14. From Marseilles to English Boxing

MARSEILLES WARMED MY HEART and my success was no longer in doubt. The two weeks at the Alcazar passed quickly.

I made two good friends there. The first of these was Bertho, the song and dance man. He soon forgot the humiliation of the three resounding "bravos" and began to smile again. You know if all the artists who failed in Marseilles should jump into the Vieux Port there'd be no room for ships there.

Anyway, I got a big kick out of Bertho's goatlike voice and did a take off of him:

> *Spr-i-i-i-ngt-i-i-i-me*
> *Subl-i-i-i-me*
> *Cra-a-a-a-zy*
> *Ecst-a-a-a-sy*

Bertho and I had a regular routine each night at the end of my act. We ran as fast as our legs could carry us to the Strasbourg Brasserie on the Place de la Bourse. There we settled down to our small beer and sausages and sauerkraut and felt like kings.

Franck, our manager, didn't usually mix with the performers, but he made an exception of me. Somehow, from the first evening, we clicked. I spent a lot of time in the hole that he called his office. And the last evening of my engagement he gave me a contract for the following season at thirty-five francs a day!

I felt very sad at leaving these two fine fellows. They were my first real friends. But we traveling salesmen of amusement have to get used to these partings.

This tour did me a lot of good professionally. My reputation began to spread in the provinces. In all the important cities with a few exceptions things went well and I ended up with many contracts for the following season at a higher salary.

Of course records and the radio and the movies did not exist at this time. You could only reach a few hundred people in an evening, so it took long years of traveling to build up a solid reputation as a vaudeville artist.

Back in Paris I made it my business to watch some of the popular foreign artists. My favorite was little Tich at the Alhambra. He introduced to Paris a new style of comic dancing. Inspired by him I began to try some clumsy tap dancing and eccentric steps. This fitted in very well with my skits. My style slowly became different from that of any other French artist and I was better known now. Some of the youngsters even began to copy me. They talked of the "Chevalier style" and the "Chevalier school."

The Scala was the most chic music hall in Paris. We went there to see the greatest entertainers of the day and it was here that I first saw Norman French. He introduced the "step dance," a real novelty in tap dancing. He dressed elegantly and his lazy manner enchanted everyone. He accompanied his patter with tap dances, glides, and comic gestures.

All of us young fellows tried to imitate him. My acrobatic training made this feat a little easier for me. My act was now a mixture of acrobatics, dancing, and comedy.

Now I was playing in luck and I couldn't begin to accept all the contracts offered to me. I had top billing in the provinces and was never without a job in Paris. My salary climbed steadily. In the provinces I now got at least a hundred francs a day and in Paris twenty-five to forty.

A certain café in the Faubourg Saint Martin was the favorite rendezvous of all the second- and third-rate members of our profession. Every afternoon it was filled with vaudeville artists, both men and women.

The top stars could not risk being seen in this spot, but all the rest of us came there to eat and drink and talk shop among kindred souls.

One evening on my return from a tour I saw at one of the tables an habitué of the place who was then on the downgrade. I had often noticed the furtive way he looked at me but had always thought it wise to pay him no mind.

But this evening (perhaps he had been drinking too much) he attacked me head on.

"Well, star of the century, so you deign to mingle with us miserable, untalented bums!"

I was taken aback by this unexpected storm and asked him if he was in shape to realize what he was saying.

That was just what he was waiting for and now he really began to pile on the insults.

The crowded café became suddenly silent; everyone was enjoying this unexpected scene. Stunned and open-mouthed I let him ramble on.

"And so, star of my rear, if you want to settle this here and now I'm your man. Come on outside and I'll deal with you properly—you dirty little braggart!"

I stared at him, my mind in a whirl. Should I accept his challenge? If I refused, my reputation would be ruined. But I just stood there as he came toward me menacingly.

I stuttered something about how I wasn't used to street brawls, that I was no hooligan, that I didn't know what had come over him. In short I was scared stiff.

Everybody returned to their cardplaying and conversation, but there were plenty of scornful glances cast in my direction.

Mother Pagès, the manager, came to my rescue: "Maurice, you're right not to fight. If you did you'd have to do it with every cur you meet. They're all jealous of you."

This ended the incident and I left for home white as a sheet. I was overcome with shame. Yes—I was a coward. I had been just plain scared. That night I got no sleep.

Now at this time Walter Stanton and Peter Brown had just introduced English boxing to Paris. I happened to know a certain dancing teacher named Stilson who was coaching a young French boxer M. Mongevin. So the very next day I told Stilson all about my cowardice and my humiliation and begged him to let Mongevin give me boxing lessons. It was essential that I learn to fight. For I could not run the risk of being insulted again without defending myself.

Every day now I worked hard at my boxing lesson. Then I sparred a few minutes with Mongevin himself. At the end of a month my teacher was surprised at my speed and dash. I took more than I gave back, to be sure, but finally I became used to swapping punches.

One evening Stilson invited me to put on the gloves with him. I accepted, expecting real punishment. He was big and fast, but not, thank God, a ball of fire as a boxer.

After a few exchanges I sensed my superiority and, much to my surprise, succeeded in giving him a bloody nose. Stilson had to admit that he was beaten. Mongevin, our referee, was jubilant.

Though my face was slightly bruised I was wild with joy. Now I was ready to return to Pagès' and challenge my enemy. By this time I had taken blows enough to realize that no hysterical comedian could really hurt me.

I planned my fight carefully. First I would block him with my left. Then, if that worked, I would attack him with my right. I aimed to give him first a bloody nose and then a black eye. Finally, if he showed signs of slowing down I would knock him cold with a "One, two" straight to the jaw.

Feverishly I waited for the hour when the café was filled to capacity. Then I spied my opponent playing cards. Taking a deep breath I entered and went straight to his table.

I touched him on the shoulder and he turned around. I was green—but it was a determined green. The room became perfectly quiet.

"Do you remember insulting me a month ago?" I asked.

"Yes—and so what?"

"Afterwards you suggested going out in the street?" My throat was dry and I spoke with difficulty.

"Yes—so what else?"

"That's all. I'm here to tell you that I've reconsidered

and I don't see how a 'so and so' like you can hurt me. Come on, you slob, we'll clear this up right now."

I heard Madame Pagès' "Bravo, Maurice!"

There was a dramatic tension in the room.

I don't know if the fellow got wind of my lessons or if my expression frightened him but anyway he backed right down and began to apologize. He said he had been drinking too much and really had nothing against me. He suggested that we have a glass of wine and forget the whole affair.

But now I was really cocky and wanted to regain the respect of all these people. So I answered calmly.

"I don't drink with a coward!"

Then leisurely I made my way to the desk and invited Madame Pagès to have a drink.

15. Eldorado

MY ADVENTURE at Pagès left me in a state of physical confusion. I had stored up so much fight that this peaceful solution was a terrible letdown. I was a little like a country which has armed itself for a war that never comes. Often in the night I would start up with clenched fists.

Needing an outlet for all this energy, I began to hang around boxing rings and sometimes was able to pick up a fight with one of the trainees. I often appeared on the stage with a swollen eye and even more "sensual" lips than usual.

During my engagement at Lille, I went to a gym run by Francois Descamps and asked if I could have a few rounds with one of his pupils. The only one who was free was fourteen-year old Georges Carpentier. But, on second thought, Descamps decided I was too heavy for Georges! I have often teased Carpentier since about the time when he was afraid of me!

I was so crazy about this new sport that I even composed a little music hall skit called "English Boxer." Dressed in striped tights and boxing gloves I put on a mock fight with myself. The critics called it "very original."

As for my love life during this period, well, troupers must take things as they come. For us it's just as natural to be a Don Juan as it is to bow before the public. Little affairs of the heart are taken for granted in our world. You do not realize until later how much of your strength and your heart have been wasted on these shabby little romances.

Looking back over my youth I regret that nobody was able to instill in me a healthier and more poetic attitude toward love. The Louque had taught me honesty and common sense, but I had to learn about sex for myself the hard way.

But in any event my home life with Mamma was ideal now. We had a still larger apartment at 118 Faubourg Saint-Martin. We managed to save half my earnings and still live very comfortably on the rest. I often brought friends home to dinner and Mamma took great pleasure in serving them.

When Mamma and I were alone, I told her about every-thing (almost) that I was doing. I sang her my new songs and taught her as best I could the current English and American ditties which were the rage in Paris. We would hum them together, she singing the melody and I the harmony.

Every night after the show and a snack at the *brasserie* (and sometimes further amusements) I always went home. I was never too late to hear the voice of my dear Louque calling good night. She could never go to sleep until I was safely in my room.

Then came what was for us truly a big event. I was invited to replace Dranem at the Eldorado during his tour of the provinces. This was a high honor for a boy of nine-teen, and furthermore it would bring in a thousand francs a month!

On the day of the dress rehearsal I felt dizzy and sick to my stomach from excitement. That evening, for the first time in my life, I was going to be the main attraction. The other stars were jealous and we rehearsed in an atmosphere of silent hostility. I was so nervous that I kept yawning all day long. Toward evening I felt a little better and decided to celebrate with a good dinner. Seated all by myself in a deluxe *brasserie* in the Boulevard de Strasbourg I ordered the three-franc dinner and a three-franc bottle of wine to go with it—this was a real spree!

The Eldorado was full to bursting when I got there. The show had started and Montel, who performed just before me, was on. I went quietly to my dressing room, more than a little tipsy from all that wine. I wasn't a bit nervous any more and laughed at myself for having worried all day.

The audience was applauding and shouting for Montel. But he refused to go out for his usual encore. I vaguely wondered why. Then I heard a stagehand say, "He's trying to ruin this fellow, Chevalier. It's a dirty trick!"

The whistling and stamping of the audience became deafening. The other artists were begging Montel to go out. Stubbornly he refused. You could hardly hear the orchestra as they started up my introduction.

I felt like a bottle of sauterne made up as a comedian. And Georgel finally had to push me onto the stage. The roaring redoubled. But I was so well soaked in sauterne that it all seemed like a big joke. I decided that the audience and I might as well play this game together. While waiting for them to quiet down I began to walk round and round the stage never stopping. We would see who'd quit first—them or me.

I didn't even feel the floor under my feet; I was floating on air. And after a while the blast calmed down somewhat. People began looking at me in surprise. I kept right on whirling. Each time I passed the footlights I gave them a wink as if to say, "We're in this together." As their attention grew I pulled my hat down over my ears and did a few eccentric dance steps. I soon had them roaring with laughter and the crisis was over. Old Montel was forgotten and I was saved again by my lucky star.

It was at this time, too, that a pretty new face came into my life. She was the darling of the night clubs, just about my age, with a haunting beauty and a warm voice with a catch in it. One moment she stirred you with songs of love and the next she had you laughing over some vulgar ditty of the streets. She was gifted from her pretty ankles right to the top of her ashen hair.

She was not my first love, but she was my first real passion. Our liaison lasted for more than a year.

Our youth naturally drew us together and it all began charmingly. She earned unbelievable sums of money and spent it all on an orgy of night life in Montmartre. I was irresistibly tempted by the novelty of all this.

She sang at Fishers', Rue de la Chaussée d'Antin, from midnight to two in the morning. Then began a round of the nightclubs of Montmartre where she was always in demand. Rich drunken revelers offered her enormous sums for the pleasure of seeing and hearing her.

She was exposed to so much vice and so much money at so early an age that it is easy to understand why before long she completely lost her head.

For a while I accompanied her on these nightly excursions, but I felt so uncomfortable and embarrassed that I soon gave it up. After that I just saw her at dinner. Then after my show I went to her apartment where she would come to me at dawn.

My reputation soon began to suffer. In the eyes of her crowd I was only a gigolo. It became more and more evident to me that I was slipping into a shady life. People began to gossip. They said that I was on the verge of ruining my career. They even accused me of accepting money from my lady friend.

But I let myself be lulled by all of this undreamed of pleasure and didn't listen to my better self which kept warning me that I was following a dangerous path.

For a time my profession and my love brought me the keenest joy that I had ever experienced.

Meanwhile, at the Eldorado, Montel continued to humiliate me whenever he could. Every evening in the dressing room he would say, "Monsieur Chevalier, you're a no good. You haven't any talent at all. You only know how to stick out your rear. Make the most of it! You won't last long."

To get even with him I would always remark loudly to

someone near by, "It sure is easy to please the public these days."

After two months of this nagging I had my revenge. One evening we spotted in the audience P. L. Flers, the producer of the Folies Bergères. We all watched him avidly through the hole in the backdrop. The next evening he sent me a letter asking me to come to see him at once. No other member of the cast got such a summons.

The following day I went home to dinner with a contract for three consecutive season at the Folies Bergères at a rising scale of 1,000, 2,000, and 2,500 francs a month. The Louque and I could hardly believe it.

16. *Folies Bergères*

THE FOLIES BERGÈRES belonged to another world. It was the most important and luxurious music call of Paris, a temple to wealth and beauty and a soft life. It had an international reputation and visiting foreigners usually went there on their first night in Paris. The immense lounge was a regular love market where armies of pretty girls strolled about displaying their charms. Both in the audience and behind scenes you saw the world's most famous men and women. As you sipped your champagne, inhaled the smoke of Havanas, and eyed the brilliant jewels and low-cut dresses of the beautiful women, you listened to nearly every language imaginable. As a matter of fact the audience paid little attention to the stage show. They were much too busy chatting and watching one another.

The director gave me a spot in the show which he put on at the beginning of the season while rehearsing the winter Grande Revue. This was a great honor, as he rarely hired French singers; the Folies was too international and specialized in visual artists such as comic dancers, jugglers, acrobats, and conjurors. The director made an exception in my case because I accompanied my songs with dances and comic stunts.

My opening song was a parody on "The Child of Love," the piece by Henri Bataille:

> *Since first I saw the sky above*
> *I've always been the child of love . . .*

Each time I repeated the chorus I jumped forward twisting my body. Heretofore this stunt had always got a laugh and established a friendly contact with the audience. But this evening nothing at all happened. Not one of my songs or dances or extemporaneous quips brought even an encouraging smile. The spectators were just plain bored.

The following evening the management put me on sooner and shortened my act. But I was almost grateful for this as I had expected to be fired altogether.

The next day Nozière, the critic of *Le Figaro,* summed me up:

"How did this slipshod gawk get onto the stage of our first music hall? Who hired this laborious and painful comedian to appear in the midst of first-class numbers? And what vulgarity—especially the song based on Henri Bataille's chef-d'oeuvre! What filth!"

I remembered the words of Montel—"You're a no good!" And realizing that I was too common for this great theater I suggested to P. L. Flers that he give me my liberty.

But he refused and patted me kindly on the cheek. You're still green, young Chevalier," he said. "But if you listen to me and follow my advice you'll be the big hit of the evening when we present the Grande Revue d'Hiver. In the meanwhile try to be more proper on the stage. Relax. Don't strain so hard for comic effects."

That was that. Nobody ever argued with P. L. Flers. He was the master. His show always brought in fortunes, and the most famous artists were crazy to appear in his revues.

Our winter show was to mark the return of Gaby Delys from New York and London where she had been a sensation. She and I were to play a scene together ending with a dance. But during rehearsal she fell ill and one week before the opening the doctor ordered her to break her engagement.

The management decided to try Jane Marnac, a young bombshell, who had just made a great hit at the Gaîté-

The Man in the Straw Hat

Rochechouart. This was quite a risk, as she was still relatively unknown.

She had only four days to learn the role, to plan the dances, and to try on costumes. But this didn't worry her at all and she just laughed at our fears. The very first night she was able to get along without her script and she tried on her dresses as she rehearsed.

Her childlike excitement at the dress rehearsal amused everyone. When things went well she laughed. When she made a mistake she laughed. And this laughter was so contagious that we all knew she was going to be a great success.

But as she took Gaby's place in my arms (I mean to say in the scenes which ended with a dance) I began to feel that all was not well.

Now Gaby was an excellent dancer and very light. Jane Marnac was full of good will and dash, but you cannot plunge into a dance like you can into a song. There is rhythm and technique and timing to be considered, and then too Jane was a very big girl. It was a great effort to whirl her around, and I was afraid I did not have enough muscle.

When we came to the dance I braced my legs and hup! —with all my strength I whirled her around.

This should have been a knockout. For in 1908 it was a real novelty to see a beautiful young girl act, dance, sing and—whirl in the air.

But at this last rehearsal, fatigue, excitement, and bad

luck caught up with me. My effort was so great that a re-sounding noise reverberated throughout the theater at the same time as the "Hup!" of the whirl.

There was no orchestra for rehearsal. Just a piano. So it couldn't have been the trombone playing a prank.

What was it then?

After a stupefied silence the rehearsal audience burst out laughing. I felt myself growing red. Jane, doubled up with giggles, pointed her finger at me. I gave her a long, surprised, and suspicious look. The laughter now became uncontrollable and no one thought of investigating further. But after that I was always terrified when we came to that part of the performance.

The revue opened well. Jane Marnac made a big hit, the stage sets were dazzling, and Miss Campton, the other woman star, gathered new laurels with her spicy roguish-ness.

The male leads were for the most part veterans of the stage and old favorites of the public. There was nobody in the world better at reciting topical verses than Claudius, that lisping old comedian from the Café Concert. Maurel, his partner, was small and round and made a perfect straight man in the scenes where they reviewed the scandals of the past year. Although I had infinitely less talent as a comedian than these top-notch performers, I managed to contribute something, thanks to the elasticity of my legs and a facility for the Anglo-American rhythms.

Being the only comic dancer of the troupe I had the good

fortune to be chosen as a partner for the women stars. I was young and strong and full of pep and this mixture of comedy, song, and dance made me stand out. Rhythm has a mysterious power and often can stir people more than any other form of entertainment.

P. L. Flers' scripts had real quality. And I was careful not to inject any vulgarity into them if I could help it. As I watched Claudius and Morton from the wings I was struck by their naturalness and delicate touch. They never exaggerated or underlined an effect. I was beginning to learn the meaning of the word "class."

Every morning I took lessons in "the step-dance" from an English dancer named Jackson. I improved steadily and became intoxicated by these complicated rhythms. Soon I found myself clogging unconsciously in the street or in a store or café.

I was infinitely pleased with my new job. It permitted me to work in Paris, in an atmosphere of luxury and pretty women. It also allowed me to live with Mamma.

Mamma and I were now able to take an even better apartment at 18 Boulevard de Strasbourg. The window of my room and that of the dining room opened onto the Passage de l'Industrie and from there I could watch the comings and goings of the whole profession. The furnished houses opposite were occupied by vaudeville artists and we talked back and forth from window to window.

We got rid of a lot of our old furniture and I bought a more imposing dining room suite and a bedroom set that had a wardrobe with a mirror. We purchased an upright piano which we thought gave a tone of artistic comfort to the dining room.

The revue went along smoothly. The atmosphere behind scenes was friendly. Compton and Marnac were kind to me from the beginning. They allowed me to loll around their cosy perfumed dressing rooms as much as I wanted. The three men stars were friendly enough, but I never got to know them as well.

Morton was even funnier behind scenes than on the stage. He never took anything seriously except the dress rehearsal and the first night. After these were over he spent most of the time trying to make his colleagues laugh on the stage. He never took his merry eyes off you for a moment, and while you spoke your part he kept coming out with the lowest of jokes, the filthiest of wisecracks. But his innocent expression never changed. No one could resist him for long, and his partners were constantly on the verge of hysterics.

This same year I was engaged by Cornuché to play in the summer show at the Ambassadeurs, in the Champs Elysées. My contract ran for three summers. I now had only two free months in the year and these I filled in with tours of the provinces.

On one of my tours of the provincial cities I came across a new music hall recruit at Lyons. Her name was Collette Willy. She was large and well rounded (the most popular type of beauty in 1908), and of course I fell in love with her right away. I was alone in Lyons, and when I wasn't watching her on the stage I thought about her constantly. But I was intimidated by her grandeur and I didn't know how to approach her.

I asked her friend Georges Wagner about her, hoping that he would introduce us. But instead he told me all about what a hard life she had had. She was working in the music halls just to earn a little money. Her real talent was for writing, he said, and this would make her famous some day.

But she did seem amused by my work. From time to time I caught her watching me secretly. Then one evening she came up to me as I was waiting to go on stage.

"Why do you look so sad?" she asked.

I didn't know how to answer. She was too imposing and I was trembling with excitement. I muttered something idiotic about not having much reason to find life gay.

She answered that I should be ashamed, that I had all my life before me.

In brief, I did not dare confess my feeling for her.

Much later I learned that during this tour she had been writing one of her greatest books, *The Vagabond*. When I read it I discovered to my astonishment that I was the character called "Cavaillon." She depicted me as a large, blond, wild-eyed boy.

We became friends many years later when she was the

great Colette. Then I confessed the feeling I had had for her at Lyons.

"Is that so, dear Maurice? How silly!" she said. "You should have told me. What a shame that I am now a fat old lady—and it's too late!"

17. Mistinguett

MY FIRST SUMMER at the Ambassadeurs was marvelous. It was wonderful to be a star performer in this place where only a few years before I had been one of the poverty-stricken crowd gathering the crumbs outside.

Each evening I strutted down the Boulevard on my way to work. The sidewalk cafés were crowded and the boulevards were alive with strollers breathing in the *joie de vivre* of Paris.

After the show I usually went on to other night spots to watch the popular actors of the time.

Max Dearly was my favorite and I went to admire him whenever I was free. He was charming, witty, a marvelous dancer, and everyone adored him. I will never forget the night I first saw him at the Moulin Rouge dancing his famous "Valse Chaloupée" (Swing Waltz) with Mistinguett. This number has since made the fortune of dancers the world over.

What a beautiful couple they were!—I left there almost sick with jealousy and admiration for Max. As for Mistinguett—I couldn't get her out of my mind. Her beautiful expressive face, her supple and desirable figure, were always before me.

Mon Dieu! I was in love again! This new love swept the memory of my first passion entirely from my thoughts. But my new love didn't think any more about me than she did about an insignificant ant.

Mistinguett was at the pinnacle of her career and I was hardly in the same world with her. She was courted by the most famous people and was rumored to be in love with a certain comedian.

It seemed hopeless for me to even get to know her, but luckily she was engaged for the next revue of the Folies Bergères! You can imagine that I counted the hours until our first rehearsal.

That day the whole troupe was on the stage of the Folies for casting assignments.

A sort of platform was placed over the orchestra pit and on it were seated P. L. Flers, the author and stage designer, the ballet master, the director, a secretary, and Mistinguett. As his name was called, each performer stepped up to the platform for his instructions.

My heart began to beat like sixty when they announced Mistinguett's scene.

"Chevalier!" called P. L. Flers.

I stepped forward.

"Good! You two are to play the main comic scene together. It's called, 'La Valse Renversante.' I will explain it."

First we had a comic dialogue, nine-tenths of it for Mistinguett and the rest for me. Then an argument, with her slapping me over and over again as she stormed around the stage. I just had to stand there and take it. Then a dance ended the scene with her clasped in my arms. In our rapture we knocked over chairs and tables. Then we whirled over the sofa onto the rug and rolled up in it entirely. Finally we unwound and, still waltzing, disappeared suddenly through the window.

You can see that this was not very delicate stuff, but it was excellent music hall. I had got this role solely because of my aptitude for dancing, my youth, and the strength I had built up by my boxing. It was agreed that Mist and I could have the stage to ourselves for rehearsing each day from eleven to noon.

There was no danger of my being late. I was ready in my rehearsal costume (sweater and dancing sandals) long before the great star arrived. She came dressed in a chic tailored suit but quickly changed into a cute work costume and our enchanting rehearsals began.

We got along well from the very start. We had both come from plain people, and the great Mistinguett easily put herself on my level. We both spoke the same language

115

—that of the Faubourgs. I could really be myself with her, for she would burst into happy laughter at my vulgar jokes. Apparently in her circle they didn't usually laugh so easily. They had too much wit and not enough natural gayety.

Our act was bound to go over well as we were relaxed together and had confidence in each other.

I had promised myself not to court her because if I failed all the fun would be spoiled. Still the hours I spent away from her were long and empty.

But one fine day, during our dance rehearsal, as we were rolled up in our rug alone together suddenly we both knew that we were in love. The unwinding was much slower that time, I can assure you.

I was just twenty-two now and still extremely naïve and timid when I found myself out of my element. On the stage or in my dressing room I was sustained by my professional success. And I felt at ease in my *quartier*. But elegant restaurants and stylish night spots gave me the cold shivers. I always felt these superior people were looking at me disdainfully. My first tuxedo might have been made of metal I felt so stiff when I put it on.

Mist understood all this and tried to cure me of this timidity. She urged me to go to all the stylish openings. But I still felt a little like a peasant who had been generously invited to the chateau.

Sometimes Mist met me in a little café on the Boulevard de Strasbourg. She didn't want people to know our relationship yet, and at these meetings she always wore a thick veil.

I realized that she had many other admirers, but I was not jealous yet. Between the Louque, my work, and the time I spent with Mist, life was full to the brim.

18. *Benefit Performance*

I WAS ASKED to take part in a benefit show for the Ris Orangis, a home for retired music hall artists. The main attraction was to be an English boxing match between a white boxer and a colored boxer. And I was chosen to be the white boxer.

Boxing was still new in France, and people were expected to come from all over Paris to see a Negro professional fight the amateur from the Folies Bergères.

But I wasn't too keen about the idea, really. To put it mildly, I was no Carpentier, and it would be easy for me to make a fool of myself.

However, the committee had planned to arrange a deal with the Negro. They would bribe him to go easy in the first two rounds and let me knock him out in the third. *This* was more like it!

117

Young Joe Glans, a good second-class professional, was enchanted to accept the sum offered. He agreed to fake the first couple of rounds. Then in the third round it was understood that I would give him a good right and put him to sleep like a baby.

The walls of Paris were covered with advertisements of the fight, and every day the newspapers were full of this extraordinary event. I was already a hero, and men and women looked at me admiringly.

Because I was so sure of the outcome I didn't even think of training for the fight. After all, I certainly had enough wind for two rounds—only seven or eight minutes.

The morning of the great fight arrived. I wasn't the least bit nervous. Emile Maitrot, the official athletic referee of Wonderland Francais, was chosen to be the referee, and my seconds were Georges Carpentier, Adrien Hogan, and Bernard, the top-notch French boxers. All of this was window dressing to give the effect of a championship match. I almost took it seriously myself.

After a good heavy lunch (why not?), I arrived at Bata-clan. The room was packed. The crowd paid little attention to the concert part of the program—they had come for the fight. They were curious to see an actor take it on the nose. They had come to gloat over blood and swollen eyes and lips—in short to spend a pleasant afternoon.

My seconds were with me behind scenes. Then I saw my Negro. He was shorter and weighed less than I did. I nodded and tried to give him a little look that showed

Chevalier at the Théâtre des Ambassadeurs, 1908.

Ambassadeurs 1908

Chevalier boxing, in 1910. This was after his famous exhibition bout with Joe Glans.

Chevalier poster in 1908.

Chevalier with Mayol, Boucot, and Mistinguett.

my sympathy. He responded coldly but I thought that was part of the game. I almost burst out laughing.

Putting on my trunks and my heelless boxing sandals I looked at myself critically in the mirror. It is true that I was a little lacking in muscle, but I had a good figure and on the whole I was well pleased with my appearance. Then, donning a very rich-looking wrapper, I nonchalantly walked onto the stage where a ring had been set up. The Negro was already there leaning on the ropes and talking to his friends.

Blithely jumping over the ropes, I caused a lock of hair to fall over my forehead. I hoped this gave me an appealing youthful appearance.

There was a burst of applause which I received very modestly. Carpentier, Hogan, and Bernard smiled as they laced my gloves and massaged my muscles (they were in on the game). The Negro opposite was now alone, and as a sporting gesture I almost offered him my seconds.

"He must be having black thoughts," I whispered to Georges. It wasn't a very funny joke.

Maitrot announced the fight and called us to the center of the ring. He warned us to fight clean and not to hit below the belt. I smiled at everyone, but the Negro avoided my eyes. What an actor! We returned to our corners to take off our wrappers. The gong sounded.

I went out to meet my adversary as if I had been prize-fighting all my life. I extended my left glove to him and he touched it with a slight grunt.

A second later something entirely unexpected happened. I was taking my time posing in a graceful position on tiptoes à la Carpentier, my chin was buried in my left shoulder and my left arm was ready. What was my opponent doing all this time? I was too busy to see. But while I was taking my graceful pose the Negro leapt at me. I felt the wind from his left glove as it grazed my jaw. As I retreated instinctively his right fist landed like a cannon ball in my stomach.

This terrible blow doubled me up. I couldn't breathe. With my head down I looked like I was searching for a coin all over the ring and I was groaning oh's! and ah's! What was *this*? A real fight?

The audience was in an uproar. Painfully I managed to draw myself up and then my man went at me again with all his strength. Automatically I jumped back and the blow just brushed me. But it had such force behind it that the wind from it made me shiver in terror.

I could hear Carpentier shouting, "Put up your left, Maurice, and defend yourself!"

I obeyed Georges automatically and managed to land four or five desperate lefts on the Negro's nose before he had time to plan his attack. That slowed him up a little. This was better, but I was still far from feeling aggressive.

As I circled around him I whispered behind my glove, "Are you crazy? You know very well what the agreement was!"

I'll never forget the expression on his dark face as he answered me:

"I'm not kidding!"

And then he leapt at me like an unchained beast.

After this it was not so much a boxing match as a foot-race all over the ring.

I had never thought that pure funk could change a man into a grasshopper. Now I'd touch him with my left and hup!—I'd be two yards away. I am not sure that I didn't jump right over him. At any rate he never found me where he expected to—I would come from the side, give him a quick blow on his nose, and disappear again into the unknown. As the first round ended he was more confused than hurt.

My seconds were furious at this treachery. Hogan (then the middleweight champion of France) went to the Negro and told him that if he kept this up he would fight him afterward with his bare fists.

But the man just kept repeating slyly, "I'm not kidding, I'm not kidding!"

The second round began. The Negro was now a little less dynamic and I defended myself with my left. My fighting wasn't very scientific. I just hit out with my left and tried to take as few blows as possible.

In the following rest period the Negro let us know that he would "lie down" in the next round. And he did, thank God! After a trembling right from me, he seemed to waver, then he collapsed. The crowd scented "a fix" and streamed out, without protesting, but without enthusiasm. I will never know exactly what happened.

But there was a rumor on the Boulevard de Strasbourg that the Negro had profited from two sides. From us and from an old enemy of mine.

19. My Fall

I WAS VERY HAPPY as the pleasant weeks and months of 1909 and 1910 rolled by.

Each morning I woke up about ten—if I hadn't been doing the rounds in Montmartre until dawn.

I had a little Chinese gong on my night table which I struck until Mamma, who was waiting in the next room, answered my call. She would come running to throw back the curtains and open the shutters. Then she'd kiss me good morning, bring me my café au lait, the newspapers, and the mail.

At a quarter of eleven I set out for the Folies Bergères to take my tap-dancing lesson with Jackson.

Then I returned to the Boulevard de Strasbourg and waited for Mist's morning phone call at the Café Guillaume Tell. It is hard to believe how excited and nervous I used to get when I used the telephone. I never braved it except in emergencies or when someone called me at the Guillaume Tell. We didn't have one at home. So I was doubly excited when Mist called me. If for some reason she failed my day was ruined.

After my telephone call I used to bound up the stairs four at a time to lunch with the Louque. This was her big moment of the day. All her love and pride went into our meal together. I always ate up everything she prepared, washing it all down with good red wine.

Then, full to the tonsils, I'd stagger to my bed and flop down for an hour's siesta. This routine seemed perfect to me. And Mamma was sure that to eat and drink heartily and to sleep right afterward was a sign of excellent health.

At three in the afternoon I went to the gym to practice boxing. First I had a lesson, then sparred two or three rounds. After this I skipped rope and finished off with a shower. At five o'clock I would return to the Boulevard de Strasbourg where I was sometimes lucky enough to have tea with Mist. Otherwise I joined my pals for an aperitive on the sidewalk of the Brasserie Psschorr and watched the crowd go by this popular corner.

Then home for a light supper with Mamma, followed by the evening show at the Folies Bergères with my two loves, the job and the woman I adored.

I couldn't ask for anything more. On the whole, my life was full of happiness and well being.

But at times I still felt like a gate crasher in this enchanting world. You see I was always afraid of losing the little bit of voice that I had. So I worked like the devil at my dancing. In case of laryngitis I wanted to be able to earn my living as a dancer.

I was also afraid of tumbling from the heights that I had reached. And it looked for a while as if this might really happen.

All of Paris was talking at this time about my old friend Boucot the comedian. Since the Concert de Commerce he had gone on from success to success, in Paris and in the provinces. And my second summer at the Ambassadeurs he was at the Alcazar d'Eté, also in the Champs Elysées. His debut there was a huge success. Everyone was crazy about him. I wasn't in the least jealous, but I began to feel very uneasy about this competition.

The morning after Boucot's debut I received a warning from Cornuché, who owned both establishments. He told me that my audience thought that I had come to a standstill. Then he urged me to go and watch Boucot that evening. So, after exchanging acts with another artist, I went to the Alcazar to sit in on my own death sentence.

Boucot came out as usual, a little overdressed and over made-up. The blond wavy wig, the red nose—a little overdone; the jacket and trousers—questionable.

He began to sing in his serious voice and this went on for some time. The crowd was getting restless.

Then the orchestra played a few bars of music and kept repeating them while Boucot very slowly and solemnly took off his imaginary gloves, rolled them up, and put them in his pocket. He began humming a tune that harmonized with the notes of the orchestra. He invented words that did not belong to any language but sounded to French ears a little like English.

> *Ouan dignenigne nousaille*
> *Ouan dignenigue mousnaille*
> *Tafalgar Square e Troufignon Street . . .*

In the second verse he mixed the Chanson des Montagnards and Lakme, still as serious as a pope.

This sort of horseplay was a novelty at that time and the audience was crazy about it.

After his second verse Boucot repeated his "Ouan dignenigue" as he circulated among the customers. Then without stopping his song he nodded to a woman at one of the tables and kissed her hand. The man with her was smoking a cigar and Boucot took it and inhaled as though to test its quality. Then he calmly snatched the woman's purse, examined its contents and looked at himself in her mirror.

This business was very daring and it was something new. As Boucot left the room the crowd was almost sick from laughing.

I went away from the Alcazar completely dazed. This looked like my finish. And at the end of the season I received a letter from Cornuché releasing me from my contract with the Ambassadeurs and the Alcazar d'Eté.

This was a hard blow for me but it was a good lesson. You see, ever since the Folies Bergères I had not bothered to learn any new songs or change my act in any way. An artist can't hope to stay on top long if he's as lazy as that.

After my release from the Ambassadeurs I made a tour of the provinces. Perhaps I was played out. The work seemed harder to me now. I drew a good audience but I had to make an agonizing effort to really get a hold on them. I was so tense that my voice gave out after the third or fourth song.

And the following winter in the Folies revue my scenes didn't go over as well as before. I was completely overshadowed by the two new clowns from the Cirque Medrano, Antonet and Grock.

I was in a constant state of anxiety and felt that everyone was losing interest in me. Mistinguett still loved me, but I was afraid she pitied me a little too. As I became more and more attached to her I also became more jealous and irritable.

My final season at the Folies was even more discouraging than the one before. The director had sent to England and America for new talent. Tom Hearn, Chris Richards, and W. C. Fields came and all of us Frenchmen took second place beside these great international stars. My contract was not renewed and it was clear that I was no longer in demand.

But I had a great stroke of good fortune. A revue by

André Barde and Michel Carré was just going into re-hearsal at the Cigale and the shortage of young male actors obliged the director to offer me the lead. I accepted like a drowning man grasping at a raft.

People began to talk about me again as though they had never seen me at the Folies Bergères during my whole four years there.

But there was a black cloud to darken my new *joie de vivre*. I had been old enough for military service in 1908, but up to now I had postponed it from year to year. Sooner or later I had to serve my two years like everyone else and it was impossible to delay it more than one more year.

20. Military Training

WEEK BY WEEK the unavoidable date drew nearer. To make my departure even more painful I had an offer for the next summer revue at the Ambassadeurs. They offered me top billing and twice the salary I got when they dropped my contract two years before. Also, Antoine wanted me to play opposite Regina Flory at the Odéon. And Régis Gignou asked me to be in his new play *L'Ingénu*.

My last evening after the show I spent first with Mist

and afterward with Mamma. The next day I had to tear myself away from this wonderful life and take a train for Belfort to join the 35th infantry.

I arrived at Belfort on December 1, 1913, and set out heavy-hearted for the center of the town. Where did they keep the 35th infantry? I finally found the barracks. I presented myself to the guard sergeant. My name obviously meant nothing to him and without changing his expression he pointed out the building of the 10th company where I must sign in.

Soon the Captain sent for me. After chatting a little about my profession, he cheerfully reminded me that a soldier's life at Belfort was very hard. I'd have to adapt myself like everyone else. I assured him of my good will and obedience and returned to my barracks.

There the men looked at me with hostile curiosity. An "actor"?—They'd soon take that out of me! I was too blue to react. First I must put on a uniform. Then get myself a clipped haircut. As I had some money, I was able to go to the canteen for lunch. The other soldiers must have thought me an unmannerly fellow for I just sat and brooded about this fix that I was in.

I have awful memories of my first trip into Belfort in uniform. The streets were swarming with soldiers. Since I was a private, I had to salute almost everyone I met. I felt like a stunned stray ant among all those red pants. The town was garrisoned and infantrymen bumped into each other at every turn. When I passed a corporal without

128

saluting, he showed me his stripes. "So—private, second class—don't we salute?" he snarled in a pronounced peasant accent. I saluted and apologized, explaining that this was my first day of military life. He gave me a hard look. My Parisian accent didn't inspire him with confidence. But he magnanimously deigned to let me go unpunished.

That evening I found the Grande Taverne, the most modern *brasserie* of the town. It seemed that theater and music hall companies appeared there from time to time. They even had a small stage in the room reserved for soldiers. I heard a muffled-voiced comedian whose neck veins swelled painfully as he tried to drown out the hum of the crowd. Then a slender young soldier sat down at the piano to accompany a pretty young singer. Why this boy had real talent!

At the end of the song he came to my table, called me by name, and invited me to drink with him. I had felt like a lost dog all day so I accepted gratefully. Now I learned that the soldier had been a pianist in a Paris night club but had won a first prize at the Paris Conservatory. He had composed the song the young woman had just sung. His name was Maurice Yvain and he said that he had applauded me many times in Paris. After gossiping until time to return to our barracks, we planned to meet for an aperitive the next day.

Because it looked as if I had at last found one friend in the army, I went to sleep under my military blankets feeling a little less like a helpless baby bird. I slept soundly until the bugle call, which got us out of bed at six. The corporal set the new rhythm with "Go on there—get up faster!" and I was on my feet in two minutes like all the others. I raced to the canteen for my coffee. My two neighbors helped me make my bed and arrange my knapsack.

There I was, in the square lined up for assembly. I looked like a fool among those young soldiers who knew what it was all about. I was hopelessly confused by the "on guards" and "at rests." The men stifled their laughter. The adjutant bawled me out and decided to have a "first-class soldier" teach me the exercises and the handling of guns.

The other recruits were at least four years younger, and I felt like an old man compared to these kids. I was twenty-five and had twelve hard years in the entertainment world.

A peasant named Lardet became my "buffer." He was to polish my gun and my bayonet, make my bed and shine my boots. In return I agreed to pay him a hundred sous a week.

He had a humble, smiling face and I took to him at once. The military profession began to seem more civilized now.

Several Parisian boys from other companies heard of my arrival. They had seen me in the cafés of the capital and they welcomed me now with open arms. "Never mind, Maurice," I thought, "this'll soon be over."

One day my adjutant sent for me. They had told him

I was a hit in Paris! "So you are an entertainer?" he asked. "How much do you make at that job?" Thinking that he was proud to have me in his company I answered modestly, "Four thousand francs a month, sir."

He stiffened. I could see that he was thinking, "A music hall artist gets all that while an adjutant—"

He smiled at me sarcastically, "All right, Soldier Chevalier, since it's a habit of yours you may sing all day long if you want to. But get along with this man now and clean up those latrines!"

But I didn't let this upset me too much. At five o'clock every day Maurice Yvain met me at the café. He was anxious to write for the opera—but first he must earn some money. We drank and talked and I gave him advice for the future.

We planned to get the newest Anglo-American songs so that he could study their unusual harmonies. For if he learned how to write that sort of thing he could make plenty of money.

So I dropped a line to Mist asking her to send the piano scores at once. Yvain and I rented a room and a piano in the town. There before dinner each evening we had time for an hour and a half of music. We planned to work and experiment. My body might be acting a little like a soldier by my heart remained in Paris. And every evening to the tune of one steps, fox trots, and rag-time, Maurice Yvain and I dreamed of the future. Our fellow soldiers began to notice us, and whenever there was a benefit concert I was asked to sing with Maurice as my accompanist.

Rich neighboring industrialists invited us to dinner now and then. After the coffee, Maurice would play a few bits from Chopin or Liszt. Then I would sing. We became quite popular and after a while we got a small fee as well as our dinner.

Our reputation grew even beyond Belfort and we had an offer for a big director's meeting at Nancy. They offered five hundred francs for me and three hundred for young Maurice. We were lodged at the best hotel and invited to dine with the André family. This was a gold mine for two poor soldiers like us.

For some time now I had been dreaming of trying my act in a dress suit and top hat instead of in a clown costume. I had a full-dress suit made in Paris at Cumberland's (!) when I was home on leave.

One fine day Maurice and I decided to try my dangerous experiment at the next Grande Taverne benefit. We agreed that if I seemed to be going over all right Maurice would stand up after my first song and pretend to look for something on top of the piano. But if I was a flop he'd stay seated.

I was very much excited that first evening because it's a big step for a performer to change the costume his public is accustomed to. But before I had finished my first song Maurice rose up as he played.

This meant that I had a new goal to aim for. There are

comedians and there are "leads," but a comic lead man is a rare bird. I knew now that my two years in the regiment weren't going to be entirely wasted. I planned to work for the future while taking my military training and I intended to bring back something new to the music hall when I returned.

But in spite of this good resolution, the weeks dragged painfully between leaves. I constantly longed for Mist. For, unlike many women whose men are far away, she remained faithful to me.

One evening the captain invited Maurice and me to dinner at his house. We were obviously expected to display our talents. This was considered a great honor. We decided to make the best of the situation by filling our stomachs and then trying to please the captain and his guests. For we thought it would be a real *soirée*.

It was nothing of the kind. The captain was alone with his plain little wife. This was a very difficult situation for a soldier in uniform.

After dinner they seated themselves in armchairs against the wall. The captain relaxed blissfully and all but loosened his belt and put on his slippers. But his wife was ill at ease and stared at the floor most of the time.

Maurice Yvain sat down at the piano and soon forgot all about his uninspiring audience. He lost himself entirely in his art.

But when my turn came I experienced one of the most embarrassing moments of my whole career. The captain's wife didn't know what to make of me at all. Once in a while she shot me a severe and uncomprehending look. And the captain looked at his wife from time to time as if to say, "Obviously that isn't very artistic, but this poor man is doing the best he can."

Maurice and I tried a few feeble jokes but we felt that the captain might lock us up at any moment for lack of respect. It was pure torture.

One morning an orderly brought the news that I was to change companies and join the 31st infantry at Melun. This was wonderful! Melun was only forty miles from Paris. Only an hour on the train each Saturday and I would have twenty-four hours in Paris. I would be able to see the Louque and also spend a lot of time with Mist.

After the cold and snow of Belfort Melun delighted me. It was spring. The military life was not so strict here. The officers smiled more often. And to complete my happiness Mist came there to recuperate from an operation. I could see her every day from five to nine. Life was almost too perfect.

There were rumors of war but I paid no attention. I have never been interested in politics. All that belonged to another world. War? How uninteresting! Since it didn't interest me, why should it concern anyone else? They talked about battles, but all I understood was love and singing. War? Ah! la la—wars were all right in their time but now they were out of style!

Nevertheless the war talk became more feverish. In Paris people got more and more nervous over the alarms.

I got a pass and went to spend a week end in the *quartier,* even though it was out of bounds. Mon Dieu, here it was! The walls were covered with placards. General mobilization! People laughed and cried and sang and shouted in the streets in an excess of patriotism.

I had to join the 31st at once. Our battalion would leave for the front in four days. I couldn't believe it.

At the barracks the officers were making patriotic speeches to the soldiers. The men were doping themselves with liquor and premature bravado.

For a moment I thought of looking for some excuse to stay behind. But no—I was in the same boat with my pals. I must stick with them. I wouldn't dare look in a mirror again if I didn't.

Of course I was not exactly frantic to be on the battlefield. I had to do my duty, but this whole thing was tiresome to say the least.

THE MORNING OF the fourth day found us in battle dress, laden like mules. The regiment paraded through Melun amid flowers and cheers. I didn't know what to think. They were taking me away from everything in the world I loved: Mamma, Mist, and the agreeable life of Melun. I couldn't even imagine what a battlefield looked like. I hoped I would be brave, if only to save face before the rest of the company. But I was ready to burst with misery as I smiled at Mamma and Mist. Then we were on our way.

The officers didn't tell us anything after that and we expected we would have to fight the next day. But day after day we camped in one village after another. We began to think we were to be a reserve and stay at the rear. This all seemed amazingly like our training maneuvers and our nerves grew calmer.

Each man chose a buddy for life, or for death. I joined up with a fellow named Parigot. He was small and almost bald. We made a pledge to help each other in case of need. His nickname was "the Mole" and I became "the Mole's father." As soon as we arrived in a village he always disappeared for a while and then came back with plenty of fine things to eat and drink. He had a real knack for arranging our beds on the straw in a corner of a barn as well as for serving our little feasts.

The regiment almost always set out at dawn, destination unknown. The 21st of August passed as usual except that we didn't seem to arrive anywhere. After doing fifty kilometers, pack on back, we reeled into Cons la Grande Ville and at once they ordered us to "fix bayonets." That very night we were expected to surprise and capture the village of Cutry which had been occupied by the Germans since the afternoon before. We had heard the guns all night but we had not realized that we were as near as this.

The order to attack affected us like a drink of straight alcohol. This was it! We were going to our baptism by fire. Silently, bayonet in hand, we advanced toward Cutry. On my left a man prayed as he marched. Near me the Mole was swearing in a whisper. I advanced heavily, too exhausted even to tremble. We stumbled over the slopes and rocks expecting to find ourselves in the thick of the melee at any moment.

Since we had been told to be quiet, there was a mournful silence as we neared Cutry. A group of scouts was sent on ahead, while we waited panting. They came back with the good news that the Germans had withdrawn a few miles from the town. Ouf! What luck!

As we settled down in the deserted town several warriors attempted a cynical joke or two: "When they heard that the 31st was coming they ran like rabbits." And "Will we have to go all the way to Berlin to see them?"

The Mole and I chose our spot and I relaxed while he went out in the dark for supplies. We wanted to celebrate this first victory even if there had been no combat. Several peasants had abandoned their houses and the Mole was able to find plenty of food and drink. God, but it seemed good to us. We each drank a litre of wine and soon forgot our narrow escape from death in a deep sleep.

At dawn Cutry had a festive air with all the men milling around in their red trousers. The natives leaned from their windows. We began to hope that the Germans would not return, and we soldiers joked optimistically as we got ready for the day.

They sent us out on patrol and suddenly we saw our first corpse. It was a German soldier, almost a boy, who looked as if he were sleeping—a sentinel fallen at his post. Oh! The war seemed more real now. We could sense the nearness of the enemy. We were in the soup for sure.

Soon after we returned to town a burst of fire crossed the village square like a flash of lightning and several boys in our company fell. *"Aux armes!"* Everyone leapt to his gun. My section was stationed behind a low wall to the right of the church. Although the enemy kept up the bombardment, the church remained standing.

We fired steadily at a gray line of troops which we now saw slowly approaching, but they were still too far away for us to accomplish much. The Germans must have been crack shots, as several of us behind the wall had already been laid low with holes in the forehead. Now only our heads rose above the wall and our caps proved a better target for the enemy than protection for us.

I reloaded and shot mechanically. All my life from Ménilmontant up to my departure from Melun was passing slowly through my mind. I had gone to a lot of trouble to wind up among these boys!

As in a dream I heard the Mole's voice. "Don't worry, Maurice, your Mole is beside you!" I patted him without looking at him.

There was an infernal racket because the artillery didn't let up for a second. Only a few of us were still firing, and now we could make out the faces of individual Germans as they drew nearer.

We few survivors had no more chance of stopping the gray-green tide than a baby has of stopping an automobile with his arm. But we kept at it.

Now the Mole told me that the order to fall back had been given. I had heard nothing. I crawled to my pack with the others. We did not dare stand up for a second in this rain of bullets.

There was an even louder explosion near the church. Then I was flat on the ground with a burning sensation under my knapsack. Two orderlies ran to me. Their faces seemed to grow longer and narrower as they approached. Their voices sounded strange and far away as they asked me where I was hit. I motioned with my head. They removed my pack and I heard one of them say, "It went right through his knapsack. If he gets out of this he owes it to that."

The other asked, "Have you the strength to crawl a little way? If we don't leave here pretty quick we'll stay forever."

I gathered every last ounce of strength. We got to a little ditch but we were not well sheltered. The enemy began to surround us and the men who tried to double back were mowed down like tenpins.

I was so faint that I didn't care any more. What would happen would happen. I saw the major, white as a sheet, giving orders that no one could carry out. My lieutenant, followed by five of his boys, started straight toward the advancing hordes crying "Onward!" Poor boys! Poor lieutenant!

Captain Rollet, who later became General Rollet of the Foreign Legion, had a bullet through the cheek but didn't seem to know it. From time to time he mopped off the blood as he gave orders for taking the wounded to the rear.

The two orderlies lifted me and we made our way down the road leading away from Cons la Grande Ville. Bullets whistled around us, but we finally came to a slope that sheltered us for a moment.

The Chateau of Cons la Grande Ville was the headquarters of the Red Cross. There they examined my wound and bandaged me up. At last I was in a bed between white sheets and sleeping the happiest sleep of my life. Whether I woke up or not seemed of no importance. I was too dead tired to give it a thought.

I slept for ten hours. Shells fell on the Chateau and bullets came through the windows and burst against the walls of the room where twenty of us lay wounded. But I did not hear a thing.

I finally woke up to the sound of hobnailed boots and guttural voices approaching. The rifle fire was dying away.

German officers entered our room, revolvers in hand. They checked to see if everyone was really wounded and disarmed.

Now we were prisoners of war.

22. *Kriegsgefangene*

I HAD BEEN badly wounded in the back of my right lung. According to the German doctors there was a possibility of avoiding an operation. If I stayed quiet and had a little luck the wound would heal. We'd see.

In the meantime I had fulfilled my duty as a soldier. I now had a good chance of saving my skin without being ashamed of myself. The war could not last more than a few weeks! With all of our allies we would surely settle things in less than two months.

I looked forward to a pleasant convalescence at the chateau. I didn't know what they planned to do with me afterward, but anything seemed preferable to the bullet in the head received by my unfortunate comrades.

The man in the next bed groaned continuously and died in a few days. It was frightful but it made you feel grateful that you were still alive. I improved from day to day. Finally when I was able to get up I was shaky, but I felt ready to face a new life.

What would this new life be?

The Germans told us to join another group of convalescents near the cemetery wall at Cutry. Everyone in our group was terrified. You see, we had heard horrible stories about what happened to wounded prisoners.

Someone said mournfully, "Yes, they're going to shoot us in a heap and we won't be far from the communal grave." Some of the men burst into sobs and called out the names of their wives and mothers. Others accepted the inevitable.

Two sentinels led us to the wall of the cemetery. Nothing happened! When we were all gathered together they marched us to the station.

We were transferred to one cattle car after another as we slowly made our way to Germany and captivity.

The trip took two days and two nights. We passed a great number of stations swarming with soldiers and officers. Civilians came to look at us, but their eyes were full of hatred. We were in a sad fix and we had been through a lot, but we still had the instinct for survival and somehow managed to hang on.

When we got off the train we were marched to Alten Grabow where we were to form one of the most important prison camps of Germany.

At first this was only a huge parade ground which was used in peacetime for army training. There was no organized shelter for the thousands and thousands of disarmed soldiers who were sent there each day. As the crowd grew, we hurriedly put up immense barracks.

There were French, Belgian, English, and Russian prisoners. We formed a curious gathering of colors and of languages. Gradually we became more organized and were separated by battalions in enclosures guarded by sentinels.

Parisians of the same *quartier* found each other and soon sympathetic groups formed. In one batch I joyfully spotted Joe Bridge, the young stage designer. We also had Aveline, the opera dancer, Maurice Chevillard, the famous aviator, and Louis Tunc, an actor from the Palais-Royal. What luck! These were men with whom I could talk of Paris and my profession and mutual friends. All of us arranged to get into the same barracks.

After a while the prisoners were able to organize a canteen with German goods. Those of us who could sing often stood on packing cases in the canteen and did our best to lighten the hearts of the others with popular tunes.

Led by the talented Joe Bridge we even managed to build a little theater with a real stage. Then we got permission to give shows there for the prisoners on Sundays. Aveline danced for us and Louis Tunc entertained us with his comic skits. The feminine roles were played by the younger boys. A kind of travesty of life was organized.

The camp became somewhat like any large town with its scandals and vice, its charms and contrasts. But the lack of femininity was painful to all of us, and to some it was intolerable.

At first we thought the war would be short and that Christmas would see us at home. As we came to realize that we were going to be locked up all winter at Alten Grabow, captivity became more painful spiritually as well as physically.

Apparently there was a rumor in Paris that I had been killed at Cutry. Later they heard that I had lost an arm in battle. But now I was allowed to reassure Mamma and Mist with postcards. My wound gave me no trouble any more and, in case of complications, we had some good French doctors among the prisoners.

Mamma and Mist sent me food packages and clothes and money orders. They wrote and told me that I must live as best I could and that they loved me and were waiting for me. Mist wrote to me every week and promised to look out for Mamma. My heart was full of gratitude for her loyalty.

Several of the doctors in the camp talked with me, as they had heard me sing in France. They decided to train me to be an orderly. After a few days of lessons I was made an assistant pharmacist of the camp infirmary. From then on I had a little room of my own at the infirmary as did Joe Bridge who was Infirmary Chief. I had a bed with sheets, instead of a pallet, and heat in winter and facilities for cooking. All in all it was a cushy job.

In the morning I was expected to care for the mild cases in the barracks. I was allowed to go to any battalion that needed my services. I and my large satchel of medicines were seen everywhere. When my outside visits were over I returned to the infirmary to take temperatures, make urine analyses, and wait for the doctor's visit.

I followed the doctors from bed to bed taking notes. From time to time the French doctor questioned me very sternly in order to impress the Herr Doctor.

"Chevalier, have you made the analysis of number 12?"

"Yes, doctor—a little albumin."

"Chevalier, have you washed number 6?"

"Yes, doctor. His fever has dropped two points."

"Thank you," the doctor would answer seriously and the visit was over. But I wasn't finished because from eleven to noon I had to give injections of gray oil to all the syphilitics in the camp. According to them I did this better than any of the other orderlies. I did it with great

145

care and compassion. They never felt the needle. First I massaged the spot with alcohol and just before I injected the needle I slapped the rear with a sharp blow. Between the slight numbness caused by the alcohol and the shock of my hand the patients didn't feel the prick at all.

There was some free time in the afternoon and I took advantage of this by learning English. You see I wanted to talk to the English and American girls in the music halls where I hoped to work after my liberation. I dreamed of their admiration and astonishment as I conversed easily in their language. Also, this knowledge would be an advantage if I went to London to study the music halls. Anyway, this task helped me to forget the abominable homesickness that attacked me from time to time.

Ronald Kennedy, a friendly English sergeant, was my teacher. I repaid him for his time by little favors that my position in the infirmary permitted me to offer.

Our situation as prisoners grew worse as the war dragged on, but I was one of the least unhappy. My job as orderly saved me from the boring daily exercises and my study and our Sunday concerts kept me busy.

During the summer of 1915 the end of the war seemed further away than ever. A second winter began and we were no longer sustained by our hopes of peace. Maybe the war was going to last ten, twenty, or thirty years. We would be in fine shape by then!

About this time a typhoid epidemic broke out and the

infirmary was filled for several weeks. The position of orderly was now a dangerous post because of the risk of contagion. Joe Bridge and I worked steadily and we succeeded in saving a good percentage of the cases.

However, I saw a number of boys die. My main effort was to prevent them from knowing that they were going. I became a kind of father confessor. Seated on their beds I talked with them about their mothers and wives:

"This won't last long you know," I'd say. "When you are well I think they'll send you home. Won't your little wife be happy to see you? And the old lady?" And so forth and so on.

Thanks to this dramatic deception, several of them died full of hope. I am prouder of this role than of any other I have played during my whole career.

Another summer came and we felt that we couldn't go on this way any longer. We were all tormented by thoughts of making plans for escape.

From time to time the belligerents exchanged doctors and orderlies through the Red Cross at Geneva. The news got around that if you could prove to the Germans your title of orderly they would put you on the list.

It is impossible to describe the scheming that followed. The next day a hundred prisoners appeared with properly stamped certificates proving that they had been orderlies before the war. The problem was to weed out the real ones. The stakes were serious because success or failure meant either departure for France or a German prison until the end of the war.

Joe Bridge and I signed up. Fifteen days later we heard the result of the investigation. These two weeks seemed like a century and we feared that the whole thing had fallen through.

In October, 1916, twenty-six months after our internment, a notice arrived saying:

"The orderlies whose names are on the following list must stand ready to be questioned by the ranking German doctor at 10 o'clock this morning."

Joe Bridge and I were trembling like leaves as our names were read out.

At the prescribed hour we were lined up at the infirmary. The ranking doctor arrived with an interpreter. He gave the first man two or three really tough questions, but the fellow answered them properly and was accepted. The second man failed. It was a real tragedy. I was about fifteenth on the list and I watched with haggard eyes. Although I tried to review the little I knew about medicine my mind wouldn't work at all. I could not even remember if the liver is on the right or the left side or if a bandage should start here or there.

When my turn finally came I was near despair. The doctor said something to the interpreter in German. Then came a sort of miracle. The doctor opened his mouth to speak but then he changed his mind. He didn't say a word! Again I looked at the interpreter. He was making a sign that it was all right—that I was on the list. What had happened? Was the doctor tired or did he pity me? I am sure I could not have answered the simplest question.

We left camp the next morning after giving away everything but the essentials for the trip.

They marched us to the station. After twenty-six months of prison the train seemed like a dream. Then the whistle blew and the dream became real. The train rolled by station after station. When we crossed the German border I broke down and cried for a long time.

We stopped at Zurich. There was the Red Cross! The Swiss surrounded us. They spoiled us. Chocolates! Cigarettes! They kissed us and shook hands. It didn't seem possible to be so happy.

As we left Zurich everyone was singing. We crossed the frontier and now we were in France. In France! At home. We arrived at Lyons and there was a reception on the platform. The train left for Paris at midnight. Bridge and I went to the Casino-Kursaal. Ah! A stage! Women! A real music hall orchestra—a visit behind scenes. We were like two peasants in town for the first time.

The Paris station was filled with officials and officers and crowds of parents looking for their ex-prisoners. Mist was there! We kissed a little shyly. In her automobile —Mon Dieu, an automobile!—we flew to my little apartment in the Rue Rochechouart. We scaled the stairs like children—there was the Louque! I had one of them in each arm. These two women were my whole life. They were there, and there was nothing more to say.

Mamma got busy in the kitchen. I was alone in my room with Mist. She was in my arms. And this moment that I had looked forward to for twenty-six months found me so moved that I could only tremble.

23. A New Start

As a wounded veteran I soon had my honorable discharge, but it wasn't easy to step back into my old life after twenty-six months of prison. At Alten Grabow we had dreamed constantly of the day when we would have a good meal. But I found that my stomach had shrunk during those years and now I didn't have the least appetite. And whenever I was among people I was prone to annoying dizzy spells. It was not pleasant being pitied so I kept to myself as much as possible.

But we had used up all of our savings and I had to get going again. I decided to try out first at the modest little Casino Montparnasse. On the program they wrote under my name "War wounded back from prison." They didn't

Chevalier in 1911.

Chevalier as a soldier in 1914
with his friend Maurice Yvain,
in the 35th Infantry at Belfort.

Reading a play. Chevalier is fourth from right, standing.

Chevalier as Assistant Pharmacist.

Chevalier and Joe Bridge.

At Alten Grabow, the prisoner-of-war camp in Germany.

want us to be confused with those who hadn't played the game like true Frenchmen.

I tried a few old songs and a few new ones that I had practiced at the camp. For this first performance I wore my usual old eccentric costume but left off the grotesque make-up. I'd become so used to singing in the barracks that this room full of civilians confused me. The audience reacted quite differently from a gathering of soldiers and I could not seem to hit the right note with them. I often felt faint; there were gaps in my memory and my voice was weak.

Then I tried a little tour of the provinces and it went even worse. I was on the verge of abandoning my career as an entertainer when one day a wonderful thing happened. I had forced myself to eat a little lunch and at the end of the meal a large camembert cheese was put before me. Suddenly I really wanted to eat! I devoured that wonderful camembert and knew that from now on I would regain my strength. The old machine had begun to work again.

By the end of 1916 I returned with Mistinguett to the Folies Bergères. The public rediscovered me and I was soon back on my feet. After this engagement we did an act together at the Cigale. Dressed in white, we danced to the American tune "Broken Doll."

Then the Cigale put on an operetta called *Gobette of Paris*. C. A. Carpentier, the author, had written a love scene in it especially for Mist and me. This was to be realistic and simple, a striking contrast to our usual act. I was enchanted! For a long time I had dreamed of playing a serious dramatic scene before the public, but had never been able to achieve it.

In our scene I was supposed to end my declaration of love with the words "I love you, Gobette." And the moment our lips joined, the lights were to go out by means of a trick that I will tell you about:

We were both seated on a sofa. Opposite us was a huge china dog with electric eyes shining straight at us. There was no other light on the stage. These two bulbs were supposed to go out when I pressed an electric switch hidden in the sofa cushions behind my back. At the end of the scene when I said, "I love you, Gobette," Mist leaned toward me for a kiss. Then, intimidated by the eyes of the dog, she would draw back and, taking a siphon of seltzer water from a little near-by table, spray the two holes from which the lights came.

Then as our lips joined I was to press the switch with my left hand and all would be in darkness. We counted on this trick to give the audience a charming surprise.

The opening night everything was going well and the operetta seemed headed for complete success. Then came our love scene. We could tell that the customers were enjoying it for they were completely quiet.

But just before the crucial moment, as I was making my declaration of love, I wanted to make sure (without the audience noticing) that I really had the switch in my hand behind my back.

I couldn't find the darn thing! So as I said my last few words of love to Mist, I groped feverishly behind me in the folds of the sofa and under the cushions. A murmur ran through the room. The people were beginning to wonder what I was up to.

I reached the fatal words "I love you, Gobette," and —horrors!—I finally found the switch all right but it had traveled to a spot exactly under my posterior. And as I made my declaration of love I looked as if I was scratching the base of my spine.

A wave of laughter from the audience killed my hopes of dramatic success. Perhaps I was oversensitive, but I cried like a baby for a long time afterward in my dressing room.

The German planes began to visit Paris in 1918. But the theater audiences soon became accustomed to this disturbance. And when from time to time the show was stopped for an announcement that the planes were coming, few people left their seats.

Finally, as the Gothas attacked in greater and greater force, orders were given for a dim-out of the city. At night all the lights were blue. Even auto headlights were covered with blue screens. And we heard that a drunkard was arrested because his nose was too red! In this blue light women's make-up took on a violet tint. Some chic

Parisiennes started to carry little flashlights to give themselves a more becoming color.

Night life in Paris became more and more hectic now. Officers, English aviators, Americans, and French soldiers on leave were all bent on enjoying themselves. So hundreds of apartments were turned into amusement places. Champagne flowed. American jazz bands attracted heroes, women of the world, businessmen, artists, and even characters from the underworld. Everyone was in a feverish sweat trying to have a good time.

Mist and I were invited almost every night to some gay party. Mist was scintillating no matter where we went, but I was too shy to feel at ease. In order to keep going I emptied glass after glass of champagne. The result was that I always returned home to the Louque completely drunk.

Since my return from the army Mist and I had decided not to live under the same roof. She stayed on the Boulevard des Capucines, where I could join her when I wanted to. And I lived with my mother.

More and more I began to seek the peace of my own home. I liked this much better than playing the role of servant courtier to Mistinguett. If she had only understood how I felt, I don't think we would have grown apart.

But then a kind of professional rivalry grew up between us, and that was even more damaging to our relationship. I loved my work and had common sense enough now to know that I must keep my own personality and at the same time keep changing just enough to hold the public's interest. This attitude was paying off, too, for my audiences seemed to find that my performance was improving slowly but surely.

In spite of her sincere love, Mist always considered me just a foil for her talent. She never thought of me as an equal on the stage, or as a rival. This saddened me as I could see no solution to the problem. I loved Mist, but I adored my profession and my independence.

But soon our personal troubles were forgotten temporarily. The Armistice had produced an explosion of joy in Paris. Now we just wanted to laugh and drink and dance.

At this time Paris was like an international fair ground. Entertainers from all over the world flocked to our beautiful city. Elsie Janis, the American artist, came to see our show and asked to meet me. She was surprised to find that I could talk English fluently and suggested that I go to London to play in a revue with her. This proposition tempted and frightened me at the same time. I told her that I didn't think I could stand comparison with the English artists.

She burst out laughing: "Well anyway you have more of one thing than any of them."

"What's that?" I asked.

"Charm!"

Quelle surprise! No one had ever used the word

"charm" in connection with me before this! In France they had sometimes said that I was amusing or full of pep, but that was all.

It was tough now to make a quick decision. I felt that I shouldn't desert Mist at the Casino and I wanted to make one more try at getting along with her before breaking off completely. So I now stalled for time and promised Elsie Janis to let her know when I made up my mind.

But things continued to go badly for Mist and me. I still disapproved of her circle. I blamed myself, for I felt that I should be very happy at the side of such a wonderful person.

But in the end I gave up, and one morning I telegraphed Elsie Janis in London.

The answer came the same day: "Maurice Chevalier—Casino de Paris—All right—Come over—Will start in four weeks in show with Elsie Janis—One hundred pounds weekly—Sincerely, Sir Alfred Butt, Manager, Palace Theatre, London."

When I announced this to Mist she said enigmatically, "Well, that's what you wanted!"

My director at the Cigale said pleasantly, "Well, Maurice, you're playing a game you're bound to lose, but perhaps it'll teach you a lesson."

24. Hello London!

IT WAS TOUGH leaving my whole way of life and setting out on my own to a country where I would be just another foreigner. During the whole trip I felt so lost, and lonely, and frightened by this bold adventure that I hardly dared look at the other travelers.

Victoria Station! Tom Hearn, whom I had known at the Folies Bergères in 1908, was there to meet me. We went to the Savoy Hotel, where the desk clerks spoke French. This cheered me up a little.

I had lunch alone in the grill of the Savoy. This place was the rendezvous of the most important actors and businessmen of London, but no one knew me there. So I felt almost grateful to the *Maître de'hôtel* for taking an interest in me. (I had met him on an earlier trip here with Mist.) He was very polite, but when I told him I had come here to play with Elsie Janis he just said "Ah!" and turned to another customer. He had lost interest after learning that Mistinguett wasn't with me.

In the afternoon I went to see my director, Sir Alfred Butt. He was pleasant but cold. We arranged to meet again in the evening at the show. Sir Alfred explained that I must study the show carefully because I was to take the place of the young English lead, Owen Nares. Also the management planned to add my boxing sketch and a duet with Elsie.

In the afternoon I took a long walk down New Bond Street, Old Bond Street, Leicester Square, Piccadilly, and Regent Street, admiring the glittering shop windows. Passers-by turned to look at the cut of my overcoat, which was pinched in after the Parisian style. Obviously I looked like a "Froggy." Feeling ridiculous I decided to get outfitted by an English tailor as soon as possible.

The blank expressions of the people in the street puzzled me. They looked as though they were strangers even to each other! On the Boulevards of Paris people always were ready to smile, so this icy London atmosphere was very depressing. And to think I had signed up for three months! I would return with a white beard for sure. How ever could I have thought of leaving Mist and the Louque and the theaters of Paris! I must have been crazy!

That evening Tom Hearn accompanied me to the Palace to see the show *Hello America.* The men in the audience were in full dress and the women wore evening gowns. Here and there I spotted a ravishing blonde, but on the whole the English men were handsomer than those of Paris and the women less attractive.

The revue began with a chorus of boys and girls that bowled me over. These were much prettier girls than the ones they sent to Paris! And the boys were well got up and clever and, above all, conscientious. The music hall seemed to be a very serious institution here. The chorus was as well trained as a line of soldiers.

Then Billy Merson came on. Well, these people could laugh, after all! They were like children. And Billy Merson was very funny. Furthermore, he was fast on his feet and had a good baritone voice. At home our comedians are usually funny but they are almost always awkward. And their voices are likely to be impossible. But this man had everything.

Elsie Janis made her entrance and was loudly applauded. She was a tall, thin girl and she moved with a boyish suppleness. Her immense eyes sparkled brightly. First she sang, easily following the syncopated rhythm. When she talked her voice had a quality I had never heard before. There was at the same time both humility and persuasion in her manner. And when she danced she was like a giant dragonfly whirling from one end of the stage to the other and from the footlights to the backdrop. There was a thunder of applause. The black suits and evening dresses were seething. What popularity! I decided this was no place for me.

Elsie Janis was entirely different from Mistinguett. Mist's charm lay in her sex appeal and her clever banter and Parisien chic. Here there was none of that. Elsie worked with the trained precision of a boxing champion. I was positive I would be completely overwhelmed with such a partner.

Afterward, in Elsie's dressing room, I felt like a country cousin. I told her frankly that I would never have dared to come if I had known that she had such talent. It was too bad that she had made such a mistake, but after all I hadn't unpacked my trunks yet. I could leave first thing in the morning. But she wouldn't listen to me. She was determined to start rehearsing on the following day. This girl really dazed me.

Elsie insisted that we rehearse by ourselves at first. How right she was! Speaking English on the stage was another story from speaking it in casual conversation. It was obvious that no one would understand me. I had the wrong intonations and I ended words on a high key instead of a low. This Elsie had the patience of an angel.

I wasn't an artist any more now—just a parrot. In both speaking and dancing I tried to copy everything Elsie did. I had to concentrate so hard that I became as stiff as a broomstick. But I was able to let myself go in my boxing sketch which was mostly pantomime. This made me feel a little better.

For two weeks we worked alone every morning and afternoon and sometimes until midnight. Gradually things became a little easier for me.

Although we got along very well together, Elsie was a peculiar girl. She had the reputation of flirting with all her leading men. But between us everything was always perfectly correct. Every evening I met her at the theater and we returned to the apartment in the Carlton where she lived with her mother. Our conversation was almost entirely professional, but the few times that it did become at all personal I felt ill at ease. We Parisians don't just flirt and let it go at that. We always expect concrete results. But Elsie never went further than a flirtation with any of her favorites. I couldn't understand her at all. It seemed so childish.

At the Palace she sang a song that seemed to express her feelings on this subject:

> *Give me the moonlight,*
> *Give me the boy,*
> *And leave the rest to me.*
> *Give me a bench for two*
> *Where we can bill and coo*
> *And no one can see.*
> *Give me a fairy look,*
> *Give me a babbling brook*
> *In close proximity.*
> *It's a very ancient game*
> *But it always works the same.*
> *Give me the moonlight;*
> *Give me the boy,*
> *And leave the rest to me.*

That sort of thing sounds pretty funny to a Frenchman! I tried to adapt myself to this point of view but I was decidedly irritated by it.

On the day of the opening I was almost crazy. When

it came time for me to go on the stage I shouted at Sir Alfred Butt, "You know if this doesn't go over I'll give up. I'm keeping one foot on the stage and one on the ship!"

It was mighty confusing to jabber in a foreign language before an audience that didn't know a thing about me and to have to waltz with all those strange girls. It didn't make sense, and I longed for Paris where I could sing before my own people. The rest of the world could go to the devil!

The audience clapped politely as I appeared on the stage to sing Cole Porter's "On the Level You're a Little Devil." I tried to appear light and airy and then I did a fast little tap dance. No one was exactly bowled over. In England the boys in the streets knew how to tap dance better than I could, and my voice was certainly not one to arouse enthusiasm. I know very well that I sing like a crow.

Then came my scene with Elsie Janis. Before each line I had to think over what I was going to say. This gave me an absent-minded expression. Elsie was a real pal and tried her best to keep me on the track. When we danced together I was so limp *she* had to lead me.

I had expected my boxing sketch to go smoothly, but by then I felt so dull and lifeless that I hardly got a laugh.

Before the end of the show I had decided to return to France the very next day. To hell with them! Volterra was right. I had learned my lesson. I should have known better.

Back in my dressing room Elsie, her mother, Sir Alfred Butt, and all the other performers came to congratulate me. In a tired voice I begged them not to kid me. After all I wasn't crazy and could tell a failure from a success. I demanded my immediate release.

But Sir Alfred Butt pointed out that he had my signature and a contract was a contract. I would have to finish out my three months. Sir Alfred smiled as he told me all this but his eyes were steely. Then Elsie kindly explained that London first-night audiences were always cold.

Although things went better after that I was ill at ease for those whole three months no matter where I was. Alone in my little room at the Savoy the ceiling seemed to weigh on me. And when I was invited out, although the people were kind to me, I just didn't know how to act in society. At gatherings of show people I felt like a nobody and my lack of education kept showing up.

But when the three months were finally over I was really a little sorry to leave England after all. I had made some good friends and spent many pleasant week ends with these half-innocent Britons. And the English audience, which is always on guard against all foreigners, was just beginning to like me better.

Back in Paris I had a part in a revue that Sir Alfred Butt put on at the Palace. But this was a failure and at the end of two weeks he had lost everything that he had made in London.

Then I started a tour of the provinces. I wanted to try my act dressed in the costume that I had experimented with at Belfort during my military service. My outfit consisted of a maroon jacket, beige checked trousers, light-colored gloves, spats, and a top hat and cane. This type of costume was entirely new to the French music halls and the people were crazy about it. Now I was a real English dandy!

25. Nervous Breakdown

I HAD PROVED in London that I could now be independent of Mist, so I returned to the Casino de Paris on condition that my name appear as large as hers on the programs and notices. But something told me that this was the last time I would play with her. Mist now danced with Earl Leslie and I did my "specialty" all by myself. The compliments that I received on my originality led her to think of me more and more as a rival, and this didn't help our relationship at all.

About this time I became very much attracted by a

glamorous brunette who was also a member of the troupe. In fact, all the men were fascinated by this voluptuous beauty from Bordeaux. Unless you were a monk you were bound to be stirred by her beautiful face and her luscious curves. She had little intelligence or refinement, but she was a born vamp. The very first time we were alone together our affair got well under way and I was soon deeply in love with her.

At the end of this show Mist left to play *Madame Sans Gêne* and I was engaged for three more revues at the Casino. Now for the first time I tried my specialty in a tuxedo. But I couldn't decide what kind of a hat to wear. The English often wore opera hats with a tuxedo, but that would have looked bizarre on a Parisian stage. A soft black felt seemed too gloomy. What if I were to try a straw hat? That would be elegant enough and would also light up my face. Dressed like this I sang "I Cannot Live Without Love" and "When There Is a Woman in the Corner." The response was so gratifying that I kept the straw hat as the trade-mark of my personality.

One fine day Gustave Quinson asked me to play in *Dédé*, an operetta by Willemetz and Christiné at the Bouffes Parisiens. Now for the first time in my life I was expected to play comedy for three hours in a row. This meant a lot of hard work, for it would be necessary to change my whole rhythm. I knew I could do all right with the songs and duets that were written especially for me. But it would be difficult to appear natural in long speeches where I was supposed to co-operate with the other actors on the stage.

I was able to learn this new technique, however, and *Dédé* turned out to be an unhoped-for professional stroke of luck for me. It played to a full house for two years. For a while everything seemed to come my way. Surprisingly, even the most important critics praised me. Prominent men and women who hadn't noticed me six months before now came to my dressing room to congratulate me. Sometimes I felt like laughing, but at the same time this success frightened me. It just wasn't normal.

The day after the opening the director did something extremely unusual in the theater. He rewrote my contract and doubled my salary. He explained that the long success he expected depended on my personality and if I was happy it would show in my work.

When *Dédé* began I was still seeing Mist nearly every evening. But I was quite independent of her and also spent as much time as I could with my beautiful Bordelaise. By the second season at the Bouffles Parisiens began I had broken off entirely with Mist. Now every evening I went out with my new friend. She loved night life and champagne. Our nights were not exactly restful!

I was on the stage three hours every day except on matinee days when I was on for six hours. By the second season the pace was beginning to tire me. I began to have

166

short lapses of memory on the stage. Instead of enjoying myself as I had up to now, I started to count how many songs were left to sing, and how many scenes must be played before the end of the evening. But I thought that this condition was just temporary and did not worry much about it.

Anyhow, there was no question of taking a rest. Besides everything else, I had contracted to make a series of four silent movies with Henri Diamant-Berger. This meant spending every day from morning to night, except for matinee days, at Vincennes working on these films. We finished *The Affair of the Rue de Lourcine, Par Habitude,* and *Jim Bougue, Boxer.*

Then we enjoyed a short period of relative quiet before beginning the fourth film. During this lull I decided to give a luncheon at my apartment and invite Max Dearly, Raimu, Martel, Milton, and several other friends.

For the occasion Martel, an old Marseillais and an expert cook, made an impressive bouillabaisse well seasoned with saffron. The rest of the meal was lovingly prepared by my own cook and we had the best wines and liqueurs that I could find in the *quartier*. We drank and laughed and drank some more. First we had Châblis, then a Hautbrion 1906, then some champagne. And afterward we had countless small glasses of Armagnac, while we sat around telling stories until six o'clock. Everything had gone perfectly, and as I shook hands with the last guest I was very happy.

Then suddenly I realized that I had drunk too much. My head was muddled and my legs were unsteady. I began to worry about my evening performance. But it was only six o'clock. If I could get a good nap, then a cold shower, I'd feel like new. I jumped into bed and it seemed to me that my brain floated up to the clouds, leaving my body right there in the Rue de la Bienfaisance. My head hummed like a teakettle. Even so I slept like lead until eight o'clock when my servant awakened me to go to the Bouffes.

I was glad that I had slept two hours. All the alcohol must surely have evaporated by now. But no! My head was still burning. It was as though my brain were bursting out of my skull and my blood were circulating backward. How strange! How the devil was I going to act and sing and dance! When I got up my feet couldn't feel the floor. I took a cold shower and that didn't help a bit. I began to feel panicky.

My car took me to the Bouffes. I now felt sure that my nerve centers must be affected. As I put on my make-up my face seemed to float away and come back again. My hands wouldn't function properly. Before going on the stage I called a doctor and described both of these phenomena and our afternoon orgy. He thought the excess of saffron in the bouillabaisse and the mixture of wines and alcohols had caused an auto intoxication so he gave me a powder to swallow.

Now it was up to me. As I left my dressing room I still

couldn't feel the floor under me. And my head was stuffed with cotton wool.

As I appeared on the scene there was laughter and applause. Urban threw me his first line. Completely confused, I answered him with one of mine from the third act. Urban's eyes widened. He gave his second line and again I answered with a line from the third act. Urban turned white under his make-up. I saw the heads of the musicians peering at me over the footlights.

I wasn't drunk anymore now. But my mind just wouldn't work. Fortunately people don't pay too much attention to the book of an operetta, but even so the audience was beginning to get restless. Urban, like the good pal that he was, went right on as though everything was fine. Then he turned and whispered my next line to me. I grabbed at it like a drowning man. He kept this up and I just repeated whatever he whispered to me. I clenched my hands so tightly that my fingernails went right through the flesh. Urban finally got me on the right track and we finished the first act without anything too bad happening. I was trembling and soaked with sweat.

The other actors gathered around and I told them all about my luncheon. I was feverish and still terrified at having come so near disaster. I had two more acts to play and it seemed to me like a century. Now I was insanely afraid of my script.

The second act started and it was frightful. I repeated each sentence to myself first and I stumbled over most of my words. I was constantly dizzy and in a cold sweat. And the teakettle still boiled in my head.

The evening finally ended and I went home in a state near insanity. I couldn't stop shaking. Already I was afraid of the mistakes I might make the following day. Before going to sleep I kept going over and over my scenes and singing my songs to myself. My mind jumped from one scene to another. My head was a saraband of words and verses.

Exhausted, I finally went to sleep hoping that the next day I would find that all this had been just a nightmare. The great artiste was in a fine state!

Oh yes! My brunette was there with me and she didn't understand my state at all. In fact she thought it rather amusing. She kept jabbering away about how fried I must have been! And she wished she'd been there when I mixed the third act with the first. She advised me not to be so tragic about it! After a good night's sleep she was sure I'd be myself again. Unfortunately the lady was just as dumb as she was beautiful. And all the time she was talking I kept going over my lines in my mind.

"But look," she said, finally beginning to get worried, "are you by any chance going crazy?"

I slept a little and then when I woke up the whole thing suddenly came back to me. My head continued to make strange noises and I was more panicky than ever about the evening performance. I was sure I'd make the same mistakes.

The whole day was an agony. I arrived at the theater pale and haggard. Although I got my lines right, I hesitated before every syllable.

Fearing a nervous malady I consulted the greatest specialists. They gave me shots for my glands and massages and electrical treatments. They put me on diets. I stopped smoking. I stopped drinking. But nothing helped at all.

Ever since that time I have always had the most awful obsession that a man who lives by his memory can have —the fear of forgetting my lines.

26. Finished?

MANY BOOKS HAVE BEEN written about people on the borderline of insanity trying to keep their balance. The most famous psychiatrists have described all the various fixed ideas, manias, and hallucinations without indicating any real remedy. Doctors go straight to the digestive system and diagnose autointoxication. If that fails they try all sorts of shots of gland extracts. Americans lay many of these troubles to dental ailments. Over there they think nothing of taking out all your teeth. But in the end medicine can only advise patience and courage. All that doctors can really say is that these sicknesses are aggravated by morbid imaginations and that people are their own torturers.

What an easy dodge! How does a morbid imagination get its start? And how does it end? In a padded cell, purely and simply. These complex mental diseases are a more terrible burden than many precise and visible infirmities. Some little congestion in the ear, in the sinus, or in the brain can upset the whole working of the marvelous human machine. They tell you that you won't die of it. In many cases, that's too bad, because these states can be as consuming as they are incurable.

I shall never know the exact cause of my breakdown. Perhaps the alcoholism of my father had something to do with it. Then, you remember, I had never been sure of myself. Ever since childhood I had been basically melancholy and shy with a strong sense of inferiority. There is no doubt that my lunch with the excess of saffron and alcohol and food let loose this violent reaction. That day I fought too hard to control myself. I am perfectly certain that in one evening I wrecked my nerves for the rest of my life. It would have been much better if I had come down with a high fever or jaundice. I would have been put to bed and cared for and perhaps that would have been the end of it. I should not have played that evening, but I belong to the school where an artist keeps going until he drops. I overforced the machine and something must have snapped, thus poisoning many professional successes that were to come to me perhaps as compensation.

I couldn't get rid of the idea that my memory might play me tricks. I could no longer relax because a gap in my memory might cause a breakdown before my audience at any moment. On the stage I thought not only of my immediate lines but at the same time I feverishly went over some line in the following scene, or the fifth line of my next song. I would close my eyes on the stage in order to concentrate better. If I ever did begin to relax, a nervous spasm would cause me to stumble suddenly over a word. Then the spasm would go away leaving my face and body covered with a cold sweat. The time I spent on the stage had always been my greatest joy and recreation. It had now become a torture.

People began to talk behind my back. They didn't know exactly what was happening, but they noticed something strange about me. Some laid it to my new liaison. Nothing could have been farther from the truth. But seeing me once in a Montmartre nightclub with my beautiful brunette caused many people to say that my depression obviously came from amorous fatigue and champagne.

We had been playing *Dédé* for a year without a prompter, but now I asked to have him brought back. I explained that I had played *Dédé* for so long that I often thought of other things at the same time and might suddenly get stuck. And all this was going on while Parisians were flocking in hordes to admire my optimism and youth and pep!

This martyrdom continued for several months and then I had to think of the show that would follow *Dédé*. Although I was as sick as a dog I had made up my mind to finish out the season. The next operetta was called *La-Haut,* and in this they engaged Dranem to play with me. Poor Dranem had been slipping fast during the last few years and I insisted that his name be put with mine at the head of the programs and notices.

Dranem's wife did her best to push him ahead of me. She charmed the director into giving him every professional advantage. The critics seemed to enjoy seeing me dominating the show less and less and commenced to praise Dranem extravagantly.

I was very unhappy. Some evenings I was afraid I would keel over on the stage. Dizzy spells were added to my mental spasms and I just could not compete with Dranem.

In our company at this time we had a pretty little brunette dancer, Yvonne Vallée, who was playing her first role. She did one dance with me. She was really ravishing, with her dark hair parted in the middle. She seemed modest and quiet and I often saw her soberly knitting in a corner of the wings while waiting for her turn to go on.

We began to talk together a little before and after our number. She had such a frank, open expression that I trusted her from the start. One day I invited her to lunch with me at Saint-Cloud and we took a walk in the park. Her company did me so much good that I asked her again, and little by little I explained to her all that was wrong with my life, with my health and in my profession.

She was also from Bordeaux. The contrast between her and my other Bordelaise made her seem even more attractive. At least she was the kind of person that I needed. She lived with her family and her modest means did not permit her to buy Lanvin dresses. But her heart was as sound as her body, which had become strong from dancing.

For the first time I was going with a quiet, simple young girl. She was the complete opposite of the glamorous ones that had attracted me up until now. All this began in secret. I did not wish to compromise her. Also I had to do something about the other brunette. Finally one evening I had the courage to break with her. Then I began with Yvonne on an entirely different basis. To tell the truth I had not come to this decision over night. I was something like an alcoholic who waters his wine while he gets over his obsession. What I needed was less passion and more love.

But in spite of this new friendship I was still miserable. I was slipping steadily in my career and I was still haunted by my insane passion for the woman that I had given up. I tortured myself with thoughts of what she would do with her new liberty.

I woke up one morning with the staggering idea of committing suicide. That would settle everything! It was much better to get the hell out of this wretched life in one fell swoop.

But I must think of the Louque. The poor old lady was still with me in the Rue de la Bienfaisance. At thirty-three I still lived with my mother! But I even found a solution for that. I would make my will and then I would have the doctor tell Mamma that Paris was too tiring for her and she must move to the country. I decided to use a revolver. It would be the most dignified and neatest way. I couldn't think of anything else.

Then one day in a fit of crying I admitted all to the doctor. He was amazed, for up to now he had not taken my complaints seriously. He said that I must quit work as soon as possible and leave Paris for a sanitarium for several weeks at least.

The doctors again examined me thoroughly and now they found that I had a chronic appendicitis that should be operated on before I left for the sanitarium. There was just a chance that this appendix could be causing my troubles.

According to my contract I was at liberty to leave the show after the one hundredth performance. I was operated on two days later. But this operation did not change my nervous state in the least. So I was off for the sanitarium at Saujon, accompanied by Yvonne Vallée. She was to return to the show immediately afterward.

176

Doctor Dubois, the head of the sanitarium, was very pleasant and intelligent. He had received my "file" from Paris and knew my whole history. His treatment was very simple. I was put on a diet. I was to have two conversations a week with the doctor. The rest of the time I was to rest and take long walks in the country. I did not believe that this sad existence would cure me. I became more discouraged than ever and one day I again tried to end it all. But I didn't have the courage and after that I was certain that I would never kill myself.

Now Yvonne Vallée, disturbed by the tone of my letters, gave up everything and came to be with me. A monotonous, hopeless life began. The doctor promised that after several months of this I could go back on the stage. I didn't believe him, but there was nothing to do but follow directions. This routine continued for several weeks, and all this time Yvonne was full of tender devotion. I was certainly a far cry from being the Maurice Chevalier of Paris!

One day the doctor asked if I would sing at an entertainment scheduled to be held at Saujon several days later. I told him that I could not do it. I was finished as an entertainer!

"You can and you must," said Doctor Dubois. "You will prove that I am right."

For a week I rehearsed my songs like a beginner. I arranged two numbers with Yvonne, because I wanted her near me to help in case of need. When the evening

177

came I presented myself to the little audience trembling like a leaf.

But once on the stage my poise returned and, in spite of my fear, nothing happened and the audience gave me a fine welcome.

I was never to recapture my old self-assurance. But at least I had regained my courage and now I decided to take up my profession where I had left off. I knew that I would carry on until I died.

27. The Quiet Life

DURING MY REST CURE I had been left pretty much to myself and I hadn't known which way to turn. So this show at Saujon at least got me started again and I was no longer tortured by the thought that I could never return to the stage. Of course that modest evening was not the same thing as appearing before the connoisseurs of Paris.

So I was still very depressed when my friend Franck, from Marseilles, came to see me. He asked me if before returning to the Paris stage I would sing for two weeks at Marseilles. He had talked to the doctor about me and wouldn't listen to my frightened protests. I finally agreed to sing two months after the signing of the contract.

While I was at Saujon all sorts of rumors circulated in Paris. They said that I had exhausted myself with vices. They even said I was a cocaine addict. It was rumored that I had entirely lost my memory and could not even recognize my friends.

When it came time for me to return to the capital I began to fear that this might be really true. Perhaps I really wouldn't recognize anybody! So I secretly went to my apartment alone to assemble what little courage I could. Then I had a happy surprise. I found that I could easily learn new songs. I so distrusted my memory that I concentrated that much harder and learned even faster than before. I again asked Yvonne Vallée to sing and dance with me and in a short time I was ready to risk myself on the stage once more.

I wanted to start where I was unknown. So I decided to go to a little movie house at Melun, where I had done my military service. When I asked the director if I could sing there from Friday to Sunday he thought I was joking. But I explained that I needed to rehearse some new songs and that I didn't care about the money.

I got through the three evenings there without any failure of memory. I still suffered as much as ever, but I was fighting. I was able to go on from town to town and finally to the Alcazar at Marseilles. My success there was very reassuring.

Then a new Paris music hall, the Empire, in the Avenue de Wagram, asked me to perform for the opening. I demanded three thousand francs, almost hoping to be refused. But they didn't even argue and the contract was signed for four weeks.

When I got to the Empire I was terrified. The room was as large as a railroad station! It was packed opening night and I was sure these people had come to see if I was washed up. I can never be grateful enough to Yvonne Vallée for the support and encouragement she gave me that night. And when I appeared the crowd gave me a big ovation. They were not all against me after all!

These four weeks beat the records for receipts of all the theaters of Paris. I was extremely tired, but I knew that I now had the will power to surmount all my troubles.

After this we went on a tour in the provinces, in North Africa, Switzerland, and Spain. Then back to the Empire for two weeks.

A short time later I was asked to head the bill in Léon Volterra's next show at the Casino de Paris! I was even able to demand ten per cent of the gross receipts with a guarantee of four thousand francs a day. What a victory!

The Dolly Sisters, those pretty American girls, were in this show. I did two scenes with them and two with Yvonne Vallée. Also I initiated my song "Valentine" alone and this was a great hit from the start.

Yvonne and I were now living in a ravishing little rented

villa at Vaucresson. We named it "Quand On Est Deux" after one of my songs. Except on rare occasions we stayed there all the time we were not at the Casino. My nerves seemed to benefit by this simple and regular life. My fears did return at times, but now I could control them.

But to be really happy it was necessary for me to live right up to the hilt. Although everyone took so much trouble to keep my life at home peaceful, my temperament was badly suited to a regulated existence. My instincts always call for more than I can reasonably stand. I am a curious mixture, having inherited both the wild side of my father, and my mother's prudence. I am forever reaching the edge of the precipice, but I always have just enough sense to keep me from falling over. (I touch wood.)

Yvonne was a good little friend, but my taste ran to more unusual women. She was too . . . I don't know quite what. She didn't have enough . . . what I sighed for.

After we had lived at Vaucresson for a while my neighbor, Victor Pauchet, gave me a kind of affectionate sermon.

"Maurice, a man of your importance in Paris cannot go on living this way. You really should marry Yvonne. People won't understand your behavior." He went on and on about it.

So I decided to propose marriage. Yvonne deserved it after all. She really was a fine little woman and she had stuck by me through my long illness. And I thought that

181

we would get along better if she would give up the stage and devote herself to our home and our future.

Thousands of little things in the theater had already begun to poison our love. We had constant scenes of jealousy as Yvonne didn't like me even to look at anyone else. But now if she would let me do my work alone without meddling I was ready to marry her.

You must understand my state of mind. Tired of sensational adventures, I had decided to live loyally with Yvonne. I had definitely said good-bye to all those easy and delicious contacts that are so frequent in our kind of life. But Yvonne and I were never separated, either at home or in the theater, and this began to get on our nerves. I could not help it if my eyes lit up when they met those of another beautiful woman. It would only last for a second, and I would quickly assume a detached and indifferent air. But Yvonne never missed things like that and a fight would break out on the least pretext.

After long discussions Yvonne accepted my proposal and one sunny morning we went to the mayor and then to the parish priest of Vaucresson. We had done everything we could to keep the ceremony secret. But the mayor's office was swarming with newspapermen and photographers and we said "I do" to a symphony of camera clicks.

The public was surprised to see me alone in a new revue. As for myself, I found my pleasure in my work doubled by my feeling of liberty. My act went over well

Pix, Inc.

Mistinguett.

Elsie Janis

The Albert Davis Collection

Chevalier adopts a new stage
costume at the Palace, 1920.

At the Casino de Paris in 1926.

and I should have been the happiest man in the world but . . .

But my life with Yvonne wasn't what I had hoped for. I didn't know who to blame. Our life together was always on the verge of becoming an inferno, and the only time I was really happy was when I was on the stage.

I honestly was faithful to Yvonne physically. And morally? . . . Why, what a silly question! Perhaps the very fact that I was so unjustly watched made me more susceptible to other women. However, I did really need her affection, and people thought of us as such a nice couple and so well matched. I had to go on pretending to be happy for them and for our own sakes.

I didn't know what to do. It was impossible to divorce Yvonne, and also I was afraid to live alone. My nerves might crack up again.

And to think that everyone who saw me on the stage was probably envious of me! I was such a gay character!

While I was on a tour of the Midi I discovered La Bocca, that ravishing spot near Cannes. Here I bought a small farmhouse with an acre and a half of land. My plan for the future was to work all winter in Paris and to rest in summer at La Bocca.

I named my house "La Louque." I don't know why artists always complicate their lives, as soon as they have some money, by buying property far from where they work. They always think that they will spend months there but they never can. Tours and water cures cut into the months of vacation. You end up by spending several weeks a year at a property which costs a fortune and causes all kinds of worries.

It would have been much better to have had a permanent home in Paris and spend my vacations in the wonderful hotels and inns scattered all over France. But I realized too late that one is much happier with not enough than with too much.

I have spent my life holding myself in. I have always fought against hordes of temptations. I have no consuming vices because I will not let any of them control me. I decided that "La Louque" could be my big vice. It would be my little paradise and I would make it a kind of temple dedicated to the one it was named after. I have always done all I could to make it beautiful.

28. *Long Live the King*

ALL SHOW PEOPLE who become at all fashionable in Europe sooner or later have the thrill of being presented to a king. But only a few of us have been asked to play or sing privately for a king who is visiting Paris. I have had the honor of performing for Edward VIII, Leopold III, and George VI and his Queen and I found them all to be charming and kind.

But I want to tell you especially about the king whom I felt in my heart to be closest to the man in the street, my friend Alphonse XIII, King of Spain.

I met him for the first time when I danced before him with Mist at a soirée at the Ritz. I had heard that the performers would be presented to the king and queen after the entertainment and I asked Sacha Guitry how I should act. Sacha explained to me that one never addresses royalty as "you." One must say "Your Majesty is too kind" and "I humbly thank Your Majesty" and "Oh yes, certainly, Your Majesty." I was very much impressed with Sacha's serious tone, and I tried hard to remember all of the variations of "Your Majesty" that he improvised to make me understand.

They told me that protocol forbids anyone to applaud until their gracious Majesties give the signal. Kings cannot clap their hands and stamp their feet and cry "encore, encore" as the audience does at the Folies Belleville. They can only look amused and clap with the tips of their fingers. The other spectators may then caress the tips of their fingers too. But they must make as little noise as possible so that the sound of the royal fingers can dominate the silence. This makes it rather like performing before deaf mutes. It is flattering but not warming.

We did the best we could in this frigid atmosphere, and

185

afterward, while we waited for our presentations, I kept repeating to myself various sentences that might be acceptable to the king. This head waiter's language did not come to me very naturally.

Sacha Guitry and Yvonne Printemps were presented first and they seemed to know their business. In fact Sacha assumed such a kingly manner and the King was so natural that for a moment I had them confused. But I had to pull myself together quickly when it was time to step forward with Mist. Mist amazed me with her ease and her natural chic. Where could she have learned all that?

Then when Alphonse turned to me my legs began to shake. I wanted to ask him for a chair. But no—that wouldn't do at all. What an idea!

"You danced very well, Monsieur Chevalier," he said.

"Yo—" I cleared my throat, "Your Majesty"—I felt so foolish and nervous that I almost giggled. "Your Majesty is too kind."

"Your dance looked so easy," he went on, "and yet, Monsieur Chevalier, it must be very difficult and tiring."

"Yo—" again a frog in my throat, "Your Majesty," I had to concentrate so hard that I always got stuck after the "Your Majesty" so I couldn't think of another thing— "Your Majesty is too—" finally I thought of another word —"indulgent."

Could I be mistaken? He smiled at me. He understood that in this stiff atmosphere I was like a fish out of water.

He was a good fellow after all! I began to smile too and the language of our eyes was better than all these conventions. His smile broke the ice and we got along fine after that. I didn't think any more about my language. At the end, however, I braced myself as if for a high somersault and said, "Your Majesty makes me very proud."

I must not have made too bad an impression because, after I had created "Valentine" at the Casino de Paris, the same ambassador invited me to sing my new song at the Spanish Embassy. Besides their majesties there would be Poincaré, Briand, and Edouard Herriot.

I explained to the Ambassador that my new song "Valentine" was not exactly according to protocol. There was a question of *tétons*.

"But no, on the contrary, that's perfect!" he exclaimed. The King will be crazy about it. *Tétons*—that's very French—their highnesses will be charmed."

The evening took place in the same atmosphere of silence as the other one had. I sang "Dites Moi M'sieur Chevalier" and got as much response as if I had been alone on top of the Eiffel Tower at five o'clock on a winter morning. However, the King and Queen did smile just a little.

I began "Valentine" and I never will forget it!

The first verse goes like this:

You always remember your first mistress.
The memory of mine is full of ivresse.

187

The Man in the Straw Hat

> One day in the rain
> Our joy was insane,
> Then we enjoyed it more and more.
> I asked her name and she said "Valentine."
> And as each day she took the Rue Custine
> I took the same street.
> Then I took her hand
> And finally I took all.

REFRAIN

> She had tiny tootsies
> Valentine, Valentine,
> And she had tiny tétons,
> Ton ton ton tine.

At that moment my eye was drawn to the corner where Edouard Herriot was sitting. Something in his expression worried me. I was awfully afraid of being considered too vulgar by these great people. And Edouard Herriot did not seem to be reacting very well to tétons. I continued:

"She had a tiny chin" (Herriot couldn't be shocked by that!)

"Valentine, Valentine" (I *knew* the Ambassador should have listened to me. He would surely be fired too).

"Besides her tiny feet, her tiny *tétons*, her tiny chin (Ah! Kings should stay with kings and commoners with commoners. The fellows in the balcony didn't frown at a poor little *téton*).

188

"She was as curly as a lamb."

All during the second verse and chorus I was in a cold sweat. It even ran out of my eyes and ears. Like a drowning man my whole life passed through my mind. What had ever possessed me to let myself get started on this? I looked with haggard eyes at all those important faces. Herriot put his head in his hands as if to say "How does he dare? What a nerve to parade all these *tétons* before the Queen!"

I didn't even dare look at the King and Queen. Their outraged expressions would have paralyzed me on the spot.

I sang the third verse with my eyes focused about a yard above the distinguished audience. Perhaps Herriot would decorate me with the award for national stupidity! It didn't take me long to disappear when I had finished. Yvonne Vallée and I started for home as if all the Spanish police were at our heels. Every day after that I expected to read of the scandal in the newspapers. In large letters it would say "Maurice Chevalier insults royalty."

One evening they announced the Spanish Ambassador in my dressing room. I was positive that he had come to make me find him a new job. For nothing good could have come of all this.

He entered as calmly as a Spaniard can and handed me a little package. He smiled and said, "With the compliments of His Majesty, Alphonse XIII."

I opened the package and there was an elegant cigarette

189

case with the royal coat of arms engraved on it. I was amazed.

"Mr. Ambassador, their Majesties are not angry?"

"But why would they be?" he asked.

"Because I shocked everyone with the *tétons* of Valentine. But, remember, you encouraged me to do it."

"On the contrary, Monsieur Chevalier, everyone was delighted. Believe me. The guests, the Queen and, as for the King (he lowered his voice as if he had a state secret) he told me afterward that he wanted a copy of that song to learn."

"But, Mr. Ambassador, why did Edouard Herriot put his face in his hands?"

"Did he do that?" he asked. "No one noticed it. You imagined things, Monsieur Chevalier. Monsieur Herriot certainly has nothing against the tétons of Valentine."

Then he left after a friendly handshake. I didn't feel normal again for at least a week.

29. Hollywood Bound

ONE EVENING Irving Thalberg and Norma Shearer were at the Casino and they asked to see me. At that time I had never heard of them. Thalberg wanted me to take a screen test. And if I was photogenic he promised to give me a contract for Hollywood. I told him that I no longer gave auditions, that people hired me or they didn't and that the idea of a test was humiliating. I honestly thought he was bluffing. After he left, Max Ruppa, my secretary, explained Thalberg's importance. So I sent Ruppa running after him with my apologies.

I had my screen test at Vincennes. I had to walk, and sit, and smile. The next day they had the showing and I was agreeably surprised to find that my face was possible for the American screen. But I couldn't reach an agreement with Thalberg. Jesse L. Lasky came to the Casino soon after that and he too thought I would have a good chance in Hollywood because I could speak English. Talking pictures were just getting their start. I showed him my screen test, which I had kept, and he gave me a contract for Paramount Studios for six weeks with options. They also agreed to pay the passage to Hollywood and back for Yvonne and me.

From that day on American publicity took over. Lasky and I were interviewed and photographed from every angle. In true Hollywood style enormous sums were spent on advertising me. Dinners for critics and actors were given by Paramount in my honor. During my last engagement at the Apollo everyone came to see the sensational person Paramount had created. When it came time for me to leave Paris farewell speeches were made by the most important people of the profession.

I felt all along that this cyclone of publicity was false and out of proportion. If I should fail, how ridiculous my return would be!

On the boat-train we found several journalists who had been assigned to accompany us as far as Plymouth. Apparently they were eager for the last impressions of the great man as he started out for America on the *Ile de France*. At Havre another crowd awaited us and they clutched and jostled us all the way from the train to the ship. I'd had a fever for several days, but I could not give up now. Sick as I was I had to play the game all the way.

They gave us the best suite on the ship. We had a dining room, sitting room, bedrooms with twin beds, and two bathrooms. Everything was buried under flowers, fruit baskets, and corsages, and all sorts of cards and messages. I had never had a send-off before, but now it seemed that everyone in France was excited because I was going to

America to try to make a picture. And there was nothing sure about it. All this would change very fast if I made a fool of myself in America!

In my tuxedo, I sat at the captain's table among the most important passengers. I was supposed to make "sophisticated" conversation. Sophisticated—there was a word that I was to hear a lot from then on. It seems that all Latins are "sophisticated." They had to explain this to me for I had never known it before. But in the future I must reek with sophistication. That wasn't really like me at all, but I was already mixed up in a lot of things that weren't like me and there was no way to stop now.

The fourth evening on the ship a concert was given for the benefit of the sailors and their families. Of course I had to sing. After the performance they auctioned off my photograph. The bidding was slow and painful. The American passengers did not seem to be at all excited about me, at least not to the point of wanting my photograph if it was too expensive.

Antoine, the Parisian hairdresser, was on board. When the auction came to a standstill he stood up and shouted, "Ten thousand francs!" As we had only reached five hundred francs that bid made a great impression. I asked him if he was crazy. He explained that he wanted to show the passengers what a really important person I was. The audience was stirred by his gesture and the photo finally brought fifteen thousand francs—a good round sum for 1928!

The Man in the Straw Hat

At dawn the last morning a tender arrived with some newspapermen and several people from Paramount who had come to welcome me. I still had a fever and hadn't been able to sleep. I kept turning hot then cold and I was afraid I would not be able to stand all this excitement.

The photographers arrived like an assault battery. They grabbed my arms and my legs. They asked for Madame. Everyone was on deck. The cameras clicked endlessly. They snapped me from all angles. There were continual smiles and handshakes and hats in the air. *Hello New York!* Yvonne was seated on the ropes and had to pull up her skirt. The photographers kept shouting, "Come on, Maurice, give us that big smile!" They were already calling me Maurice! This went on for at least an hour.

Then we had to face the interviews. Back in our suite a dozen newspapermen kept asking us questions. What were my political opinions? I had none. I had never even read an article on the subject. Did I think France would pay her debt to America? I didn't even know France owed her anything. That answer made the reporters laugh.

All this while the Paramount representatives kept busy serving drinks. Champagne and liquor flowed. Everyone was taking advantage of being on board ship where there was no prohibition. After each question we all took another gulp. After a while everything seemed very hazy.

I finally went out on deck completely done in by my journalistic trial. The dock was crowded and for a moment I was afraid that all these people had come just to see me. But I soon realized that they were friends and relations of other passengers.

Finally Yvonne and I were rushed in a car through the swarming crowds and noisy traffic and reached the apartment reserved for us on Central Park. For the next two days we saw all that we could of Broadway, and Paramount gave a large banquet at the Waldorf Astoria.

Then after five days on the train we arrived in Pasadena. The interviews and greetings began all over again. At Los Angeles there were photographers all over the place. *Hello everybody!* They wanted me to put my arms around Yvonne and look loving and jaunty both at the same time. There were twenty-four pretty young girls in shorts right there in the station. Adolphe Menjou, Lili Damita, and other film stars were standing before a huge canvas that said "Welcome to Maurice Chevalier from France." There was a lot more handshaking and gushing and flowers. A band played "The Marseillaise." I felt that this was going too far and I was terribly embarrassed. But I had to play the game and I kept exclaiming "marvelous" and "wonderful!" This was all so different from anything I had known during my whole career. My face ached from smiling.

Soon after we were settled in Hollywood we were invited to a large dinner given by Paramount at the Ambassador for two hundred Hollywood celebrities. Douglas Fairbanks and Charlie Chaplin were to speak. Also Hearst, who had just returned from a trip to the Continent. Then I was to sing three or four of my songs.

After dinner Hearst stood up and began to tell about his trip. It seems that they had not treated him very well in France. Calmly, without raising his voice, he poked all sorts of fun at the French people. He took them apart piece by piece. Everyone in the room was very much amused by his humor on this subject. That is, everyone but me, who had to sing in French right afterward.

I didn't know what I should do. Should I say that I couldn't sing after my country had been criticized like that? Or should I take it all as a joke? Or perhaps I should sing on my knees.

I decided to act as though he had done nothing but praise my native land. First I explained my songs in English, then I sang them in French.

I had done the right thing. Everyone soon forgot about Hearst. These people seemed to like me and I was off to a good start in Hollywood.

30. "The Most Expensive Artist in the World"

WE STARTED RIGHT IN making *Innocents of Paris*. We had to work at night as at that time the studio was busy with "silents" during the day. But I had gone there to work, and if they wanted me to work at night that was all right with me. And after the first week the studio took up my option. I was delighted, for this would make a good impression in France. At least I wouldn't have to go back a complete failure.

In this picture I had the role of a young ragman. This was the plot: One evening as I walked, singing, along the bank of the Seine I saw a poor woman throw herself into the river with her child in her arms. I plunged in and succeeded in saving the child but the mother was drowned. I adopted the child and took him to live with me in my garret.

In the course of the film the child was supposed to be overcome with grief at the memory of his mother. I had to put my arms around his neck and console him. Finally to distract him I put on a soldier costume and sang a song called "Dites-moi, Ma Mère" (Tell Me, Mother). He was to stop crying, look at me in surprise, and then finally join me in singing and climb on my back shouting with joy.

We had not been working long before I learned a professional lesson from this six-year-old child actor. When we came to the part where I put my arm around his shoulder and spoke to him tenderly the cameras stopped and the director said we must do it over again. This happened twice and I finally asked what was wrong.

The director explained that the child was taking advantage of my lack of experience in the movies to use an old Hollywood trick. He kept moving just far enough away from me so that I had to turn to speak to him and, whereas his whole face would show on the screen, only the back of my neck would be seen.

I couldn't believe that an old veteran like me was being buffalloed by this small child. After the director had given him a good talking to we started again. And, sure enough, the boy slowly moved just enough so that I had to turn my head. Once more the director cried "stop," and the child looked at him innocently.

Once more we got to the spot where he was sobbing. I put my arm around his neck. And, as I spoke tender words in English to him, I clutched the neck of that little beast with all my strength and thus managed to get through the whole scene with at least my profile showing.

Innocents of Paris was not considered a very good picture, but my personality seemed to "click" with the Americans and the song, "Louise," that I introduced soon became one of the most popular songs in the world.

Before my next picture we went to New York where I appeared with Paul Whiteman and Helen Kane at the Ziegfeld Roof. This gave me some good publicity. Then I returned to Hollywood to make *Love Parade* with Jeannette MacDonald. *Love Parade* made such a big hit that the studio tore up my contract and tripled my salary.

For seven fantastic years I lived in the hurly burly that is the life of a popular movie star. We traveled constantly back and forth between Hollywood, New York, and the Continent. Everywhere we went it was the same thing: ovations, receptions, crowds, and autograph hunters. I couldn't appear in public without some kind of a demonstration. I was swamped with offers from all sides. Yvonne and I had a few weeks vacation at La Bocca each summer. But the rest of the time that I was not making pictures I was appearing in the music halls of New York, London, Paris, or Marseilles.

All the fuss that the public makes over a movie star is very flattering and it was hard for me to keep my balance amid this hysteria. But I did not take it too seriously for I knew that as soon as my films began to make less money it would all be over.

I felt sure that the tremendous amount of publicity that I was getting would only irritate many people. But there seemed to be no escape from it. A stage actor can sometimes have a little privacy but a movie actor has none. I was not suited to all this noise and bluff. It took all the fun out of life. I knew very well that I was not worth all this racket.

When I went to London one summer I realized the power of the screen more than ever. A few years before I had caused no excitement at all. But now I was received at Victoria station by a crowd of thousands of people, who had to be held back by a hundred bobbies on horseback and many more on foot.

They led me to a microphone. I was asked to say a word to the crowd which stretched out into all the streets near the station. Yvonne's arms were filled with flowers and I smiled right and left trying not to leave out anyone.

I was embarrassed by the reception and spoke a few idiotic words into the microphone. They were greeted by thunderous applause. Women shouted and some even fainted. "Dear old Maurice!" "Hello Maurice!" "We love you!" "Darling Maurice!" It was a nightmare!

I was to appear in a revue at the Dominion Theater. The city was plastered with posters advertising me as the "highest-paid artist in the world." To me this was frightening and in very bad taste. It would not put me in a very sympathetic light with the public. Just try and make people laugh after that! The producer didn't have to appear alone in a tuxedo and a straw hat!

I always was embarrassed by the enormous sums that I made during this time. People no longer asked me,

"How much do you earn?" They asked, "How much do you save?"

Some of the Paris newspapers considered such huge sums of money scandalous. They pictured me as a vulgar clown who counted his millions each morning and then hid them away.

But I was not as rich as some thought. Two thirds of my money went in taxes. And of course my expenses were much greater than they had ever been and I had to make many contributions.

People have always talked about by economy. But after all it isn't a crime to be saving. It's in the French temperament. And surely I have a right to put aside something for my old age.

One day in London my business manager came to me.

"Maurice," he said, "I know that you are tired out from your work and all these interviews and invitations. I want to protect you as much as possible, but George Bernard Shaw has asked to meet you at once. Aren't you impressed! You don't look as if you realized your good luck!"

It is true that I was not very excited by this news. Of course I knew that George Bernard Shaw was a great writer. But he was too great for me, and I felt as though an interview with him would be something like trying to pass an examination on a subject I knew nothing about. And as I had a matinee every day, I would have to go before lunch. But my manager explained that if I didn't accept this invitation it would be an affront to all of England.

Everyone soon heard of my great good fortune. The newspapers talked of George Bernard Shaw and Maurice Chevalier. Our names were bandied about as though we were a team of acrobats.

The big day arrived and I went to his house near Picadilly. There I was before the great man! How handsome he was! He held out his hand and I muttered something about being enchanted and honored. Then I could not think of anything else. This was not one of my good mornings for conversation. There was a silence and then he began to talk. He explained that he had read so much about me in the English newspapers that he wanted to know this Frenchman who could excite the English to such a degree. He wanted to see for himself what I had that could break through the well-known iciness of the London audience.

So many extraordinary and unexpected things were happening to me these days that nothing surprised me much. But this handsome man was pretty awe inspiring.

"Listen, Monsieur—" (he hesitated as though he couldn't remember my name)—"you are a good fellow and I am going to talk to you frankly. I never go to the theater or the movies. I know nothing about your style. I don't even know whether you are a baritone or a tenor. I hope you won't hold it against me, dear Monsieur —" (I had to remind him of my name) "but, as a writer,

I was curious to see you. Now tell me a little about yourself."

I felt suffocated. The smile froze on my face and I didn't know what to say. For a moment I thought he was making fun of me. Then I saw the twinkle in his eye and suddenly I understood the funny side of the whole thing. I laughed right in his beard.

I wanted to say, "Ah, Monsieur Bernard Shaw, how easy you make things! How I like your frankness! Now I can tell you that for my part I have never read one of your books!"

Things were still not going so well with Yvonne. She was bored in Hollywood. She saw Mary Pickford from time to time, but she seldom went far from the studio. She usually stayed in my dressing room, or came to watch us working, or paced up and down outside. In a word, she did everything she shouldn't have. It would have been much better if she had made friends in the town and we could have been together only after my work was finished. As it was, we were always on top of each other. There is a kind of camaraderie among studio people that she could not seem to understand. No matter how fond you are of a person you need a certain amount of freedom.

But I hardly dared to speak to other women at the studio. At the time that we were making *Le Petit Café* Marlene Dietrich had a dressing room next to mine at the studio. How beautiful she was! But I had to be very

203

careful not to show my admiration. That would cause endless jealous scenes with Yvonne.

Then one winter she had to stay in Paris for an operation and could not join me in Hollywood for several weeks. So I was alone and free and could look around a little.

Soon Marlene Deitrich and I became good friends and we were together all the time. Of course people gossiped, but they had no reason to. Our friendship was just a pleasant distraction from our work.

Then one day Yvonne arrived. The angry scenes began all over again. Marlene broke off our friendship because it caused too many complications. But I just could not go on any longer being watched every minute, and Yvonne and I both said things that were beyond repair.

We had tried hard but we had failed. She was still young and pretty and talented, and she left with my best wishes and the assurance that she would be provided for for life.

One evening in New York I sang at a benefit at the Metropolitan Opera. Claudette Colbert and I were making *The Smiling Lieutenant* on Long Island at the time. I was very much depressed all that day but I blamed this on my nerves and stage fright. I felt feverish and faint the whole time I was on the stage and decided to see a doctor the next day.

But in the morning I was awakened by a cable from Paris. Mamma was dead! It was the worst shock I had ever had. Half of my purpose in living and working was suddenly gone. For days I could only sob. I did not know that a man could have so many tears.

I tortured myself by going over and over our whole life together since the Rue Julien Lacroix. And to think that I had not even been there to say a last "Adieu" to my poor old Louque. But I had to go back to *The Smiling Lieutenant* and work and smile and be "cute."

In the course of one year I had lost my mother and let my wife leave me. I was now all alone to face the life of an international cinema star.

The people of Hollywood were kind to me, but they were so different from the Parisians. It was very difficult to adapt myself to this new way of life. There were many people that I greatly admired, but I did not have many real friends.

My best friend was Charles Boyer. I had met him in France several times but I had never got to know him well there. He had seemed to belong to a different world from mine, for in France there is a cleavage between music hall artists and real theater actors. The latter are educated people, but in my time most music hall artists were not. I have known many who were completely illiterate. We were closer to circus people. Real actors were likely to be disdainful of the *café-concert*.

But now in Hollywood, at a time when I was lonely and shaken, Charles Boyer offered me his friendship. I liked him more every time I saw him and found that I could

205

talk with him on subjects that usually found me speechless. Finally we were together almost every evening. He seemed to know everything and to have read everything. He had all the education that I had missed.

At forty-three I became a student. Charles made lists of books for me and I read everything he suggested. When I traveled we wrote long letters to each other and I told him all about my progress. Reading brought me joys that I had never known before and I will always be grateful for the friendship of this man.

Then I did have one real "American pal." If you were to ask me who, among all the Americans I knew, meant the most to me I would answer at once Douglas Fairbanks. Americans have never had a better ambassador of good will to all parts of the world. With his sunny smile he made friends wherever he went.

Doug made you want to be an American. He was the essence of kindliness and strength and humor. For fifteen years he represented the friendly, the honest, the protector of the weak. He was what every man wanted to be.

His jokes were sometimes hard for a Frenchman to understand. But that was logical. The American philosophy naturally produces a different sense of humor from that of our country.

Doug played a joke on me one day that left me literally breathless. Perhaps I was wrong. Like everyone else I have my peculiarities and I do not always agree with others about what is funny. I'm either tickled or I'm not.

And I have often looked around an audience and noticed that while some people are rocking with laughter there are others who don't bat an eye.

Anyway, every Sunday in Hollywood we gathered at Pickfair, the Fairbanks estate. After luncheon and a siesta there was tennis and swimming. This was right up Doug's alley. He would go through his whole repertoire of fancy dives from the diving board and even from the roof of the club house. Everyone loved it.

One of those afternoons I stood on the edge of the swimming pool dressed in a stylish gray-flannel suit, the latest thing from Picadilly. Suddenly Doug leapt at me like a Tarzan and put his strong arms around me.

"What's the idea, Doug?" I gasped.

At first I thought he was just trying to scare me. But not at all! Without my being able to do a thing about it he threw me right in the water, head first. As I went under I could hear a tempest of laughter.

My first thought was for my expensive London suit. It would be ruined. My silk underwear was not so serious. But my platinum wrist-watch band—! And my buckskin shoes from MacAffee! Buckskin was meant for the woods, not the streams. As I sank I made a complete inventory of my tie, my socks, my garters, and my braces. None of them was made especially for the water.

As I came to the surface, my expression must have been a little like that of Hamlet's ghost.

Doug was almost crying he was laughing so hard. I

207

couldn't think of a thing to say as I got out of the water. I looked just like a wet dog and I felt chilled. I began to worry for fear I would get pneumonia or pleurisy, and that would interfere with my work.

At this point Yankee wit and French humor just weren't in accord. But this trick was clearly very funny to the Americans and I made a big effort to join in the fun. I said to myself "How funny this is!" But I couldn't even force a smile. My whole nature was against it. I had known too much poverty to find anything funny in ruining a fine flannel suit just for a practical joke. And that wrist watch had been coveted for too many years! All my nerves cried out against this needless waste. To me it was like lighting a cigar with a five-thousand franc note. I just don't understand the pleasure in those things.

I agreed with Doug when he slapped me on the shoulder and said, laughing, "Maurice, you have no sense of humor!"

How right he was!

But even so I didn't have many French friends like Douglas Fairbanks. Bless his soul.

One day an unforeseen and severe disagreement, the first in my seven years in Hollywood, broke out between Irving Thalberg and me. It all started when I tried to get the director of MGM to engage a good friend of mine, Grace Moore, to play opposite me in *The Merry Widow*. She was singing at the Metropolitan Opera at the time. She had tried the movies once or twice but had never been a great success as she was a little too fat for the films. But she had dieted and lost the extra pounds desired by the experts. She was undeniably attractive and had one of the prettiest voices in the world.

But I insisted in vain. Lubitsch and Thalberg said she wouldn't go over, and once again they chose Jeanette Mac-Donald to play opposite me. Jeanette was obviously beautiful and talented and I had absolutely nothing against her. But we had made three films together and I thought we both needed new partners.

However, I finally agreed to this and once more we were successful. While we were working on this film, Grace Moore had been engaged by Columbia Pictures to make *One Night of Love*. It was a sensation! In a few weeks she became the queen of the box office. I couldn't help teasing Thalberg about it.

I made *Folies Bergères* for United Artists, and soon after that Irving Thalberg, with whom I still had a contract, called me into his office.

"How would you like to do a picture with Grace Moore?" he asked.

I smiled, thinking perhaps he was joking. But he meant it. I assured him that nothing would give me greater pleasure. He went on to say that our two names together would create a sensation. There was just one little detail to settle. He would have to borrow Grace Moore from Columbia and they insisted that she be top star of the film.

"Do you mean to say," I asked, "that her name will be above mine?"

"Yes."

"My dear Irving, you know that isn't possible. My contract says that my name is always to be put before any other male or female star."

He tried to make me understand that I was being childish. He pointed out that the main thing was to make a good picture and earn lots of money. I answered that I had never been second on any bill since I was twenty years old and that I would rather be first at the Casino Montparnasse at five francs a day than second at the Palace Theater in New York at a thousand dollars. To him this whole argument seemed silly. But to me it was very serious as I realized how precarious fame can be in Hollywood.

I refused to change my position and submit to what I considered an injustice and a professional lowering for no reason.

Finally I was able to break my contract, and thus my American career came to an end. I was always uneasy in America except on the stage or before the camera. I just did not fit into the daily life. Everyone seemed more intelligent and more unself-conscious. I am sure it was my own fault, as the people could not have been friendlier or kinder to me. But I couldn't breathe in the atmosphere. I tried very hard, but I guess I just wasn't "sophisticated" enough.

210

31. The Calm Before the Storm

AFTER A VACATION at La Bocca and a tour of the provinces to try out some new songs I went back to the Casino de Paris and it was just as though I had never been away. I had been afraid that the people would have grown tired of that old face under the straw hat. It had been given so much publicity for the last seven years. But the public welcomed me with as much enthusiasm as ever and I was very happy to be back.

One evening I went to see the French version of *Broadway*. One of the lesser roles was taken by a young girl whose stage name was Nita Raya. She was very beautiful and she acted with true simplicity. For the first time since my return from America I was deeply attracted. When I met Nita I found her as modest and intelligent as she was beautiful. I had never known anyone like this before! She was so young that there hadn't been time enough yet for the stage to wilt her charming freshness.

But she was only nineteen—and I was forty-six! However, such age differences are more common in alliances among stage people than in those of other professions. Perhaps it is one of the privileges of entertainers to stay young longer. And after all I wasn't Methuselah!

But I had sworn to myself that I would never again go in for marriage or for serious affairs. I had had enough of all that. I planned to spend the rest of my life on my job, a few good friends and my responsibilities (I had founded a nursing home for music hall artists and I had been made honorary president of Ris Orangis).

However, it soon became clear to me that I could not possibly live without this refreshing child. And so Nita and I set out together on a new adventure.

The months went by serenely. Between engagements at the Casino de Paris Nita and I went on a tour all over Europe. Nita was the most wonderful companion imaginable and life would have been perfect if it had not been for the forebodings of the coming conflict. Politics was raging and demonstrations and strikes were becoming more and more frequent. Except for the Paris Exposition all that the papers talked of was Anschluss and political complications.

Paris was swarming with foreigners. The night spots were packed. But this kind of gayety was abnormal. It was all a little hysterical. Everyone laughed too hard. And how they danced! This was the time of the Lambeth Walk and there was something almost grotesque in the way people went at it. This whole period was like the sea before a hurricane when the clouds gather and great waves begin to beat upon the shore.

Although politics had never interested me in the slightest I now began to read the papers and listen to the radio like everyone else. Hitler shouted and threatened, but some of us still thought he was just bluffing. How tiresome it all was! As if people who weren't professional politicians didn't have enough to worry about! But no one would leave you alone. If you agreed with people they were ready to die for you. But if you didn't, you were treated like a criminal.

Between all this and my constant work on the stage I was tired out. In England and America the minute a man gets too much on his mind, hup!—he's off for a week end of tennis or golf or fishing. So I said to myself, "I'll pretend I'm an Englishman and have a golfing week end at Nice and forget all my troubles."

If you care for golf at all you are crazy about it. The little white ball is like a woman. It can make you very happy and it can cause great suffering. At Nice I was determined to think about nothing but the game of golf.

So one fine day I arrived in Nice, put on my sweater, and rolled up my slacks. I have always thought that golf knickers make a man look as though he were going to the dogs. I prefer to give the bottom of my trousers a double roll.

Arriving at the links, a caddie took my clubs. This kid

213

wore a nice happy smile on his face. My drive went off a bit to the right, but that didn't upset me. I was soon going to show this diabolical jade who was master! As I walked along I breathed deeply of the marvelous air. How fine it was to think of nothing but the ball and the clubs and the beauties of nature all around me.

Then the silence was broken:

CADDIE: Monsieur Maurice, I have seen you often in the movies.

ME: Ah!

CADDIE: What was that last film you made?

ME: Look, boy, that's not important, you know!

CADDIE: I can't seem to remember! Let's see—in that picture you were in love with a young girl.

ME: That often happens in a movie. Do you want to be a help to me? Then let's forget it. I came here to put all that stuff out of my mind. Do you understand?

CADDIE: Ah!

ME: Yes, little boy—

CADDIE: You're funny.

In silence we went on to look for the ball. But the kid didn't have his mind on his job and I had to help him find it. He handed me an iron. I could tell by his expression that he was about to say something and this distracted me so that I missed the ball altogether.

Making a great effort I conquered my nerves and succeeded on the second swing. We were off again.

Jeanette MacDonald and Maurice Chevalier in *The Love Parade*.

The Paramount in Paris at the first showing of *Parade d'Amour*.

Georges Carpentier, Douglas Fairbanks, and Chevalier in 1926.

CADDIE: Monsieur Garat and the others were here a few days ago.

I said nothing.

CADDIE: But they didn't have any luck with the weather.

ME (being kind): But they were able to do their work just the same?

CADDIE: Yes. But they had to make all their scenes in the one afternoon that the sun was out.

ME: Well, you see, it all came out all right. So let's not talk about it any more, shall we?

As we walked along, the warm sun shone full on my face. My next shot carried to the green about forty inches from the hole.

Getting into position to putt, I could feel that the caddie was excited. He kept quiet, but just thinking about him made me miss that ridiculously short putt. Then taking a deep breath I started grimly for the second tee.

CADDIE: Monsieur Murat was here for the movies a week ago. He had us all in stitches.

ME: Gr-r-r—

CADDIE: Yes, in one scene he was supposed to play golf but he didn't know how. He thought he could learn in a quarter of an hour!

ME: Ah.

CADDIE: Monsieur Murat has a beautiful wife. She goes to Ollivode (Hollywood!). I'd sure like to go to Ollivode!

ME: Why?

CADDIE: Because I could begin as a caddie and perhaps
be like Valentino some day; first an understudy, then
a great star.

ME: Well, perhaps you'll do just that. Let's not talk any
more, eh? Let's play golf!

The caddie began to daydream. We really were a comic
pair. I was trying to forget everything but golf and the
kid was trying to do just the opposite.

ME: Oh look! Isn't that the Duke of Windsor over there?

CADDIE (without interest): Yeah. He's been here several
days.

I stopped and watched the Duke go by on the other
fairway. He looked so young. I liked him. He had great
charm. I had been presented to him one evening in London. What a stir that had made in Ménilmontant.

Now as we passed each other I stopped and, standing
at attention, with my face as serious as a judge, I raised
my cap high in the air. I must have looked like a scarecrow! He didn't recognize me. He just waved his hand
and walked right on. Feeling foolish I once more set out
toward my ball. Now I wasn't thinking about golf or about
the caddie either.

CADDIE: Why doesn't *he* go in the movies?

ME: Now look—

CADDIE: Are you going to Ollivode later?

ME: !

CADDIE: I just asked because if you are going to Ollivode

you could take me with you. We get along so well together.

That was the last straw!

Handing him a double tip as a sort of apology for quitting I marched myself off the links.

32. *1939-1941*

IT WAS SUMMER of 1939 and the Riviera was seething with crowds of bewildered people. They were all wondering if there really would be a war. I myself did not believe it. I was still sure that Hitler was bluffing.

One day the Duke and Duchess of Windsor did me the great honor of inviting me to lunch at their villa. Afterwards we played eighteen holes of golf at Cagnes with their great friend Major Medcaff. The Duke must have recognized me after all that day on the links.

During lunch we heard over the radio that the Germans had invaded Poland. We were all stunned. Of course that meant that England and France were in the war. Now golf was out of the question and I left as soon as possible for La Bocca to discuss what we should do. Nita and I decided to return at once to Paris.

On the road we kept passing troops moving toward the Italian frontier. And there was a great confusion of vehicles of all sorts. The faces of the people were sad and gaunt. They were nervous and bad tempered. Obviously they had little enthusiasm for this war.

In Paris the atmosphere was a little better. In spite of everything, you saw people smile and you heard them telling jokes. We were advised to get gas masks at once. The German radio had warned us that a hundred planes would visit the city that very night.

After a brief lesson in the use of our gas masks and locating a shelter near our house, we went to bed early with our equipment laid out on a chair near by. We were soon awakened by that mournful and terrifying siren. We got up and dressed and then tried to remember what we should do about the gas masks. I thought that we had been told to put them on before going out.

As Nita and I nervously pulled on our masks the sirens kept wailing. How strange we looked—like two ghostly deep-sea divers! Rushing past the amazed concierge, we scuttled down into the cellar of a neighboring house large enough to accommodate about twenty people. We were the first there except for two tenants who stood with their masks in their hands, looking at us nervously. Although Nita and I were finding it hard to breathe, we stood quietly in a corner watching the others arrive. But they all were carrying their gas masks under their arms so I realized that I had misunderstood the instructions. But I didn't want to admit that I was wrong, so we endured the discomfort as long as we could. Then, just as I was signaling Nita to take off her mask, a man opened the cellar door and shouted, "Gas alert!" Now everybody calmly put on his diabolical apparatus. But since by this time we were about to die of suffocation, Nita and I took ours off. Everyone stared at us. I guess they thought we were crazy. And they must have been sure of it when, a moment later, because of our desperate need for air, we left the cellar to see what was going on in the street!

In the days that followed Paris gradually became organized for the shock that never came. The siren blew from time to time, but soon no one paid it much attention. It became the custom to bolt the shutters and to black out the lights and everyone got used to waiting.

So the winter of '39-'40 slipped by and Paris suffered very little from this "phoney war." At the Casino we played to a full house every night. Everyone was confident that France was well fortified and that all she had to do was to hold on. Of course we understood that terrible things were happening in Poland and Austria. But Parisians don't really care about anything but Paris. Those of us who aren't politicians pay very little attention to the rest of the world. And an entertainer's profession is his whole life. If we *have* to fight for France or die for her we are ready to do so. But the rest of the time we just want to

219

be let alone. I guess we feel that we are doing our share by giving laughter and gayety to the nation.

Then one morning in the spring of 1940 the news burst upon us. A full-scale offensive had begun! This was not such a "phoney war" as we had thought. But civilian morale was still high in Paris. After all the nation was well prepared, the French, the British and the Belgians were all ready, and we'd soon show the Nazis!

However, the Germans kept advancing. Each day that they drew closer to Paris there were fewer people at the Casino. Those who stayed on in the city lived in a kind of nightmare. If you talked about the progress of the Germans, you were called a defeatist. We just tried to hang on and do our job the best we could.

But by the end of May there was no audience at all at the Casino and just a handful of performers, so one night we had to close up.

At dawn next morning Nita and I got out our little Fiat and joined the columns of unhappy people leaving Belgium and the north of France. Unlike many of them we did have a refuge to go to. We had been invited to spend the summer with a pair of dancers, Myrio and Desha, who had a house in Dordogne, a district east of Bordeaux.

In this delightful country spot we soon had a large household. Besides the four of us there were Joe Bridge, Felix Paquet and his friend Maryse Marly, Nita's parents, Myrio's mother, and one harassed servant.

Everyone had to make himself useful. Some went to get supplies on foot or by bicycle. My job was to saw wood. We had no coal or gas or electricity, or even any running water. But still the life we led was charming and pleasant and, above all, we could relax for a little while.

During this time the Germans were making gigantic strides toward Paris and the Italians were advancing in the South. By lying flat on the floor and putting an ear to our ancient little radio we could get some news. But the stations kept fading out, and anyhow all these horrible events were strangely blurred by the peace and quiet of our surroundings.

As the Germans drew nearer to our refuge we became more nervous. All day long now we saw the French armies retreating down the roads. The soldiers in the army trucks had flowers behind their ears and waved to the women as though they were acting for a film. Obviously we'd never stop the Germans like this. Compared to World War I this seemed even more nightmarish. Finally I got so jumpy that every time I heard a motor behind me I was afraid it might be an enemy.

If the Germans did appear, we planned to explain that we were only an inoffensive group of artists, wanting no part of this conflict. You see, some of us were not entirely "Aryan," and we had already heard many horror tales about the Gestapo.

One day over our little radio came the announcement that Marshal Pétain had asked for an armistice. Then the instrument faded out almost altogether, as if even it was ashamed of the news. We could hardly believe our ears but consoled ourselves by saying that the Marshal must know what he was doing. After all, he was a military genius!

In a short time France was divided into two zones. After deciding to stay in unoccupied France, we went to La Bocca to spend the rest of the summer at La Louque and make our plans for the following winter.

Cannes was swarming now with all kinds of refugees. Everyone was busy discussing whether to stay in the free zone or to return to Paris. It was rumored that the Gestapo was everywhere, and that made you nervous. You had to be very careful about what you said because you didn't know who might be listening.

Then important theatrical men started coming to the Riviera, trying to persuade the stars to return to the capital. They worked on me and promised that the Germans would leave me alone. As further bait they said that the Parisians couldn't understand my attitude. But I had to look after my little band of "not quite Aryans," and I saw no reason for rushing off to Paris.

About this same time I also had many cables from Broadway and Hollywood. However, I felt that my place was at home among my own people. Our little group kept very busy for a time. Soon we were able to organize a company to tour the free provinces. Although the trains were packed with bad-tempered people and there were many delays and breakdowns we managed to get to hundreds of little towns, many of which were unknown to me before. And then there were the benefits given at Nice. We took in huge sums of money because many refugees had brought with them all they owned and they did not care how much they spent. This was the time when traffic in all sorts of jewels and valuable possessions was at its height.

But after a while the Paris newspapers began to attack me for not returning. They asked why I tarried so long in a luxurious vacation spot. Now I was in a miserable state of indecision. For, while I didn't want to co-operate in any way with the occupying forces, I also did not want to lose touch with my own people. After all, this war might go on for twenty years. Most of the well-known artists had already returned to the capital. So in September, 1941, I decided to go to Paris for just a few weeks' engagement at the Casino de Paris.

There was a big turnout at the Paris station to welcome me back. But that same night Radio Paris, which was of course German-controlled, blasted me in no uncertain terms. The commentator said it was indecent for Paris to welcome a man who only a short time before had sung before the King and Queen of England. "Doesn't he know that things have changed in France?" the commentator asked. (In the years that followed I was asked many times to speak on the radio, but I always refused.)

I begged the newspapermen not to question me about

politics. So right off the bat a reporter from *Le Petit Parisien* asked me what I thought of Pétain. I didn't know what to say. "The Marshal?—the Marshal?" I stuttered. "Well—I am against war like everyone else, and I think there should be better understanding between different peoples." I thought I had got out of that spot very well, but two days later *Le Petit Parisien* appeared with a large photograph of me and the headline "Maurice Chevalier, the popular performer, preaches collaboration between the French and the Germans!" The reporter came to me that night and apologized. He said the article had been trumped up by the editor-in-chief of the paper, who was working hand in glove with the German propaganda machine.

To offset this bad publicity, and with the aid of some newspaper friends, I got an article published in *Comoedia* protesting the fantastic statements being put into the mouths of new arrivals to Paris. I explained that we children of the music hall were only too happy to leave the responsibilities of public affairs to the chiefs of state.

My first appearance took place in a benefit at the Ambassadeurs. In one evening we made over a million francs for war prisoners and for my Ris Orangis. After this I started my short engagement at the Casino. Of course we could not turn away the German officers, but the audience was only about a quarter German anyway. The French gave me a big ovation. The Germans were polite but reserved. I succeeded in ignoring them and pretending they

224

were not there. I sang to the French part of the audience and the eight weeks passed without incident.

Life in Paris was unbelievable. Many people who used to seem like loyal Frenchmen now embarked on all kinds of schemes with the forces of occupation. They said that there was nothing else to do, and they were always trying to trap well-known persons into seeming to be on their side. Any invitation to lunch might be an ambush. I had to watch my step every minute.

While I was in Paris I was officially asked to go to Germany to sing for our prisoners of war. And the Germans urged me to accept an engagement at the Scala in Berlin. But I declined this engagement and I also refused to sing for the voluntary workers in Germany. But I did agree to perform just once at Alten Grabow, where I had been a prisoner myself in World War I. In return for this, ten prisoners from Belleville and Ménilmontant were to be restored to their families. It was understood that this trip would be given no publicity.

Arriving in Germany incognito, I spent a touching afternoon at Alten Grabow. But then a group of German artists led by Emil Jannings approached me. They wanted to give a reception in my honor and in return I was asked to poke a little fun at the English. I managed to wiggle out of this request, but I decided never to venture on such a trip again.

After making sure that my ten prisoners were in Paris, I went back to Cannes. But a few days later, in spite of our agreement, the newspapers of both zones published long articles on my visit to Alten Grabow. And not one of them mentioned that I had gone to only one camp for just one performance. Without actually saying so, they implied that Maurice Chevalier had visited many prison camps and made a tour of the German cities as well. A London paper even announced that I was pro-Nazi and went on to say that I had sung everywhere in Germany except in the prison camps!

After that I decided to stay as long as possible in the free zone with Nita and her parents. To distract our minds Henri Betti and I began to write new songs. "Le Chanson du Maçon" won the prize for the most popular song of the year. And we performed in all kinds of little places. This was better than being in Paris because people in the free zone paid no attention to German propaganda about me. They understood very well the advantages I could have reaped by staying in Paris.

33. Between the Gestapo and the Maquis

In DECEMBER, 1942, after completing a second short engagement at the Casino de Paris, I decided to give up the stage entirely until all of France was free once again. I couldn't do my job with any relish when every move I made was given a political twist.

The Italians now occupied the Riviera, so Nita and I spent long, monotonous weeks with her parents at La Bocca, just waiting.

Then we heard that German occupying forces were going to replace the Italians. Of course the Jews and political refugees were in a panic. Life had been possible under the Italians, but as soon as the Gestapo and German army took over it became a complete nightmare. Brutal arrests were daily, almost hourly, events in every town and village.

The authorities were everlastingly after me to sing for some cause or other. The government in Paris invited me to perform at all kinds of benefits, and friends kept urging me to return to Paris. They told me that I was still being criticized there for my hostile attitude and that the consequences might prove serious to me and my little group of

227

refugees. But I refused all these requests on the pretext that I was too ill to perform.

We dreaded the sight of the Gestapo's black cars prowling the streets all day and all night. I was very much worried about Nita's parents because they were traveling with forged papers. With the aid of the local police I was able to hide them in a secluded section of Nice. But if the Germans had got word of their whereabouts, the local authorities would have been powerless to help them.

I was worried about Nita too. The commissioner in charge of Jewish Questions had ordered a new investigation of her. Every time the telephone rang we shuddered.

Now the Gestapo became interested in my long retirement. They could not understand my repeated refusal to take part in entertainments. They talked of having me examined by German doctors. By this time I really was ill from worry. If I had to go before the commission I could truthfully say that I was having the same kind of dizzy spells and lapses of memory which I had suffered twenty years before. But anyway I felt certain that I was right in refusing to co-operate.

The atmosphere surrounding us became more and more terrifying. People talked of nothing but the latest arrests. We heard that many of the young people on the Riviera were in the pay of the Gestapo. Now I knew that I would rather die than sing in such a France!

We listened to the London radio secretly at night. Then we could hear the straight of things in France and we were given hope of better things to come. Every evening a French song writer who had only recently escaped to London listed the names of notorious French collaborators. One evening in February of 1944 I was amazed to hear my name among people of our profession supposed to be working with the enemy. The broadcaster promised that all of us would be punished when the proper time came.

This was the worst news I had ever received in my life. I could only keep repeating, "This is awful—this is awful." I thought of the millions of French people who must have heard this stab in the back. And I had no way of defending myself! If only I could explain exactly what had happened! My friends and neighbors knew that the song writer was lying, but the French people might believe him.

Everyone in Cannes soon heard about this broadcast. One of the heads of the resistance movement got a message through to the broadcaster saying, "Mistake on Maurice Chevalier. Maurice has given proofs of his loyalty and will give more." My name was omitted from the lists after that. But the mischief had been done.

Terror continued to reign in Cannes. Finally a friend of ours, at great risk to himself, took Nita's parents to Dordogne. And Nita and I followed as soon as we could. We left at night in a troop train containing just one third-class compartment reserved for civilians.

For a while we were all able to relax a little, because the Germans didn't bother much about this secluded spot.

But soon we heard a great deal of talk about the local Maquis. They had just formed an effective group whose chief was called "The Sun." They were supposed to be hiding out in the neighboring forests. We heard tales of night executions of peasants who were accused of collaboration. And many trains were derailed near by.

Now I not only listened for the Gestapo but I was afraid that the men of the Sun Maquis might have heard that London broadcast. And after all, these people didn't know me personally.

I made a short trip to see my doctor and get a certificate of bad health. While I was there Dordogne was declared a forbidden zone by the Germans, because of the activity of the Maquis. My friends advised me to stay in Paris, but I could not leave Nita and her parents alone when the Gestapo might appear at any moment.

Soon after I got back to the country came the great news of the landing of the Allies. Immediately the order for rebellion spread through all of Dordogne. Weapons came out of hiding places. Groups of people appeared from the forests singing and shouting with excitement. I saw a hunchback waving a gun that must have been a hundred years old. Peasants of all ages joined up with the Maquis. Even the police and the prison guards revolted.

Crazy with joy we legged it down to Mauzac to listen to the post-office radio. Then suddenly a man and woman rushed in. "Monsieur Maurice—Monsieur Maurice," they

Maurice Chevalier, Claudette Colbert, and Charlie Ruggles in
The Smiling Lieutenant.

Chevalier and his wife (Yvonne Vallée) en route to America in January, 1931.

Chevalier and Charles Boyer on board the *Ile de France* in 1933.

La Bocca, Chevalier's home near Nice.

The kennels at La Bocca.

With Charlie Chaplin at La Bocca.

Pix, Inc.

Chevalier's Paris apartment.

Wide World Photos

Chevalier with Marlene Dietrich at
the Paris Stage Door Canteen.

Pix, Inc.

Chevalier and Nita Raya at the Casino de Paris.

shouted, "don't go back to your house! The Maquis are looking for you—and they're going to shoot you!"

In a flash I thought of that London broadcast. And I knew I would not have much chance with the Maquis on a day like this. But I didn't like to run away. My face was so well known that I would have had a hard time hiding anyway. But finally I decided to go to some friends at Cadouin for the night. There we could discuss what I had better do.

I sent a message to Nita and worked my way on foot the eight kilometers to Cadouin where my friends welcomed me. Apparently they didn't believe that I was in any danger. But they put me up for the night and the next day Nita arrived. I learned that no one had gone to our house to look for me, but now we were all nervous and we decided to stay at Cadouin. Our kind friends secretly sheltered and fed us for several weeks.

There were still a good many Germans around. They were burning and looting and murdering. Our friends had sheltered a group of the Maquis and we were in constant fear of reprisal. One day the Germans burned a whole town just three miles from us.

The Swiss, London, and Paris radio all announced my death. They said I had been killed by the Maquis. My name was even listed at the town hall among those who had been executed. The German broadcast sounded like this: "The voice of Germany—Paris. Little by little the details of the death of the popular Maurice Chevalier are coming

231

in. Recognized on the street by a group of patriots, he was arrested by them. He was beaten to death with blunt instruments and brass knuckles. His only crimes were singing in France during the German occupation and going to Germany to take a little comfort to our prisoners."

After that I didn't know where I stood. When I looked in the mirror my shirt looked like a shroud to me. Perhaps I was really dead and didn't know it.

One day three armed men drove up to the house in Cadouin. I heard them say to my hosts, "He's here. We know it. We have come to arrest him. Give him up or it will be too bad for *you!*"

Because I was afraid they would harm my hosts I appeared at once. My three captors looked more curious and surprised than threatening.

"We have an order to take you to Périgueux for questioning," they said. "You must come with us."

I begged a minute's grace in order to make myself as presentable as possible and to pack a few things in case I was held overnight. Then the four of us left in the car.

By this time the news of my arrest had already spread throughout Périgueux. When we arrived at our destination a crowd gathered in front of the building. And as we climbed the three flights men and women poured out of all the rooms to look at me. I was much relieved to find that very few of them wore hostile expressions. One man even came up to me and said, "I am very sorry to see you in this situation, Monsieur Maurice."

Finally we reached a room where an officer with the rank of commander stood in the center of a group of men. They all looked at me severely so I started to talk rapidly. This commander seemed very human. His face relaxed. He told me that he would be very happy if my declaration was confirmed by the resistance committee in Paris. It seems that he was a native of Ménilmontant too and so he wished me luck. After they made me sign a statement, I thought I was through for the day. But, no! They said I must undergo another interrogation by a young giant whom they called "Captain Double Mètre."

In the car the three boys had talked about Double Mètre as though he were the big chief. They had said "Double Mètre orders this or that" and "Double Mètre never fools."

The great man entered the room and the commander introduced me by saying, "Here is Maurice Chevalier. He must sign his statement for the National Resistance Committee. Then while we wait for their decision we might as well let him stay at Cadouin."

Double Mètre smiled as he listened. I was fascinated by his appearance; he was too tall and too fat and too pale. His limbs seemed all out of proportion. He had too much of everything. He smiled even more broadly as he answered the Commander, "All right, we'll treat him with all the respect due his position."

I suddenly realized that his smile was not the good omen that I had thought it was at first. He was poking fun at me. The commander left and I was alone in the room with Double Mètre, who now stared at me coldly. He obviously hated me. In fact he was so overcome by a desire to hurt me physically that he could hardly breathe.

"Two months ago," he said, "we would have had the pleasure of exposing you ourselves. We had orders for traitors, like you, who have been condemned to death by the courts of Algiers. You know, don't you, Monsieur Maurice Chevalier (he was now panting with fury), that you have been condemned to death? But unfortunately we are no longer allowed to execute the death warrant without a superior decision from Paris."

I looked Double Mètre in the eye as a man must look at a wild beast just before he is devoured by it. I almost expected him to throw himself upon me. I had seen just such a cruel expression in the eyes of a German agent one day in Cannes when he was arresting a Jew.

Trying to hide my agitation, I said quietly, "I don't understand why you are speaking to me so severely, Monsieur."

He became even paler. He took a deep breath and shouted furiously, "Not *Monsieur!*" He showed me his stripes—"*Capitaine!*"

Then he began questioning me and I had to repeat everything that I had told the commander. But Double Mètre didn't seem to hear or understand what I said. He kept frowning fiercely at me as I talked.

When I had finished he made several insulting comments and began to dictate to me the statement that I was expected to sign. I concentrated with all my might for I must not let him twist my testimony to suit his ends.

Now Double Mètre began to dictate:

Perigueux, September 14, 1944

Before me, Captain Double Mètre, Chief of the Department of Exoneration, has appeared Chevalier, Maurice, music hall entertainer, arrested by our service at Cadouin, on evidence issued by the London radio and in the execution of a death warrant issued by the Tribunal of Free France.

I the undersigned Chevalier, Maurice, certify that I quickly realized when the government asked me to sing in Germany for French prisoners in December, 1941, that they were trying to compromise me. For the recital, instead of a fee, I demanded that ten prisoners be freed and this was promised. I certify, and this can be proved, that that was my only trip to Germany. German and French propaganda seized on this one performance and transformed it into a tour. I protest, for I did not make a tour of Germany. Since that time I have never sung at any affair that was connected with politics. For four years I have refused to make a film.

The proof that I was not in the favor of the Germans is that I have never had more than my share of gas. (Double Mètre had twisted this sentence. What I had actually said was that I had not had a car or gas and had never asked for either.) And that I used the subway in Paris and a bicycle in Cannes.

Since the German occupation I have only sung for six weeks

235

in Paris and since 1942 I have never appeared on any Parisian stage. In April, 1943, I completely retired from the stage and stayed on my property at Cannes.

Myself and my proof are at the disposition of the Resistance.

I signed the paper and waited. A photographer came and they posed me against the wall between the portraits of Stalin and de Gaulle. I stood very stiff because I was afraid I might collapse. I'm sure I looked just like "the man who is about to be shot."

Then the room filled with men and women. Some asked for my autograph. Double Mètre said heavily, "No unseemly demonstration!" When I was free to go, he refused to send me back to Cadouin by car. It was fifty kilometers away. "Get there any way you can!" he shouted.

Of course I knew that if I appeared alone on the roads or on the train I would be in danger at the hands of overzealous and fanatical patriots. Luckily I secured a lift from the man who had spoken kindly to me before the questioning started. Double Mètre did not like this at all, but there was nothing he could do about it.

The next morning another car arrived at Cadouin. To my relief it brought Nita who had been in Toulouse and knew nothing of my arrest. She had seen René Laporte who was the director of the liberation radio. And he had introduced her to a colonel who put a car and two armed boys at our disposal, with the order to bring me back to Toulouse.

All this was like a bad movie. I just had time to pack

my bag and we were off. The boys had a paper to show at all the barricades we must pass on the way. It said that they were required to bring to Toulouse a passenger who was "not to be identified." I shrank back as far as possible in the car and grimaced to camouflage my face. But no matter what happened now, at least I'd never again be at the mercy of the dreadful Double Mètre!

Toulouse was only a hundred kilometers away, but it seemed like a different world. Fortunately I had several good friends living there who understood my situation. And Nita and I were put up by a relative of René Laporte.

But even here I didn't dare leave the apartment. I just looked at the street through the curtains. Every day the radio announced the arrest of more collaborators. Almost all of the stars of the entertainment world seemed to be suspected.

Nita fetched her parents and brought them to Toulouse. How happy they were to be free of the threat of the Gestapo. The two old people walked the streets all day long smiling at everyone they passed. Now it was I who was the persecuted one. Only it was the French themselves that I feared. If I appeared in public I would be risking my life nine times out of ten.

I had got word to Ruppa, my secretary in Paris, that I was being sheltered in a large city by René Laporte. Then a sympathetic English journalist went to Ruppa and begged him to find me. He wanted to interview me in person and put my story on the front page of the *Daily*

Express. By checking the whereabouts of René Laporte, Ruppa was able to find me and one day he arrived at our apartment with several English officers. He explained that these were aviators and journalists who wished to help by divulging my true story. Much moved by their confidence in me, I talked and talked. Finally they left with a long article and a statement which I signed.

Two days later the radios of all countries mentioned this interview and told a little of my story.

Then one morning René Laporte brought to my hiding place my former London radio accuser. It seemed that he now wanted to help me out of this tragic situation. I really didn't feel that I could shake hands with a man who had done me so much harm, but René insisted that I see him. If he would retract his accusation publicly on the radio that would be a big help to me.

So one day I stood face to face with the man who had caused me such bitter trouble. As he shook my hand I didn't know what to think. Then little by little I told him everything that had happened. At the end of our conversation he asked me to give him a signed report of all that we had said and he would take it personally to the Comité d'Epuration in Paris. As he left he looked me straight in the eye and said, "I like you very much, Chevalier!"

I wonder what he would have done to me if he hadn't liked me. It seemed strange that the man who had started all this trouble now had it in his power to exonerate me.

Soon Ruppa came to Toulouse again. He arrived in an

English plane with a man from Paramount News. They wanted to make a film of me! This was too good to be true. I could hardly believe it. At last I was to have a chance to defend myself publicly.

With my heart full of gratitude for all their kindness I embraced the Laportes; then Nita, Ruppa and I took off by plane for Paris. France looked so beautiful and peaceful from up in the clouds. The English pilot circled slowly over Paris and then over the Eiffel Tower, enjoying my excitement. The Paramount News man took pictures of me from all angles. I felt like laughing and crying both at the same time.

Nothing really bad could happen to me now. I was home among the Parisians, my own people. I felt sure that they would never disown me.

34. *Public, I Love You*

WE WENT TO my own apartment to continue the film for Paramount. They let me explain for the newsreels how German propaganda had completely distorted the facts of my visit to Alten Grabow and that this was the first chance I had had to tell the truth. I ended my spiel with one of my old American songs called "On Top of the Rainbow."

The very same day Louis Aragon put at my disposal the columns of the newspaper *Ce Soir*. He had headed one of the literary resistance groups on the Riviera and it was very helpful to have him on my side. The next evening *Ce Soir* published on the front page a long article in my defense.

That evening a meeting of newspapermen was held at my house for the sole purpose of discussing the lies that had been circulated about me. These men told me that on Sunday there was to be a great parade at the Père-Lachaise Cemetery. They insisted that I appear in the parade and show the people of Paris that I had nothing to fear. Aragon was so set on this that I agreed to do it.

Marlene Dietrich, bless her, saw the article in *Ce Soir* and came to my place at once. She was in uniform because she was in France to entertain the American soldiers. She assured me that all my friends in Hollywood and New York had never believed that I was a collaborator. Mon Dieu but it was good to have pals coming through for me like this!

When it came time for the parade I felt very nervous at the idea of showing myself in the midst of a crowd that would number hundreds of thousands of people. I would certainly be a good target for anyone who considered me a traitor to France. There was no way of knowing what the attitude of the people would be.

240

At the cemetery entrance I joined up with the group of writers, students, and actors who were waiting to take their place in the huge parade.

What a mob there was! Many people turned to stare at me but they did not look unfriendly, thank God! I began to hear, "Oh, there's Maurice!" and "Well, well he isn't dead after all!" and "Hello Maurice, it's good to see you!" Some people even grabbed my hand and men raised their hats in friendly salute.

Slowly and solemnly the parade got under way. Section after section entered the cemetery. Our group was greeted by wild applause.

I walked slowly, pale with emotion. Because I was allowed to march with all these heads of the Resistance I knew that the Parisians were not against me. There was not one unfriendly incident. All along the way people called out, "Bravo, Maurice!" and "I knew he was loyal to the people!" and "There goes the son of a workingman!" "Long live Maurice!" "Long live Ménilmontant!" A crowd of friendly admirers followed us all the way back to the center of Paris.

This was surely the proof! Not one person in the street had reproached me.

But the reaction was not long in coming. Some newspapers viewed my presence in the parade entirely as a political move. They insisted that, like many artists at that time, I was taking advantage of the sentiment of the hour. And when I was called before the Judiciary Police

241

at the Quai d'Orfèvres these same papers pounced on this bit of news to spread all kinds of rumors. Also Radio Paris was dead set against me this whole time.

My reception by the police was much less embarrassing than I had expected it to be. They did not really think I was guilty of collaboration. They only wanted me to reply clearly to all the accusations that had been made against me. I did this and had no trouble at all convincing them of my innocence.

But my trials were not over yet. A letter was forwarded to me from Toulouse. It was from my song writer who had not heard of my return by English plane. He said he had read my statement to his friends on the Comité d'Epuration and they were very sympathetic. They didn't really have anything against me, he said, but they had to keep face before the public. I must now make a new statement to the press in which I would admit my wrongs. I was to say that I had made certain mistakes but was very sorry now. He would then countersign this statement and read it over the radio. In a word, he was ready to be generous and do his best to regain for me the affection of the public.

I telephoned him and explained how I had left Toulouse in an English plane. I told him about the article in *Ce Soir* and my part in the Père-Lachaise parade and my interview with the police. Obviously this statement for the radio would only be an anticlimax. The poor man seemed quite embarrassed and not at all happy at the turn of events.

After that I decided just to ignore my attackers. None

of the people I cared about seemed to think there was anything wrong with me. So, while waiting for the Comité d'Epuration to clear me, I sang for the Maquisards who were quartered at Melun. And I was also given permission to perform for the American soldiers.

Finally the Committee said that they would be satisfied as soon as they got a retraction from the song writer. At last one day he went to them and the Committee immediately wrote an official letter to the Minister of the Beaux Arts saying they had nothing against me and I could go back to work. But they were very thorough and investigated every single rumor they had received about me. And it was a full year before I got my final papers of complete exoneration.

During this year I sang for hundreds of benefits. I started out with a performance at the Folies Belleville for the charities of the Resistance. Then I agreed to sing at a fête for working girls at Luna Park. It was here that I really regained my self-confidence. There were between twelve and fifteen thousand people at this event and everything went wonderfully. I felt sure that if ever anyone was going to attack me they would have done it there.

I was determined to win back the popularity that I had had before the war. I sang for galas in Grenoble, Marseilles, Cannes, Nice and even Lyons, the headquarters of the Maquis. And I was well received everywhere.

Since we had been back in Paris Nita had changed a

great deal. Her youthful spirits had been repressed for too long and she soon lost the childlike charm and natural gaiety that had sustained me through the long years of the war. She went back on the stage and became intoxicated by the glamorous life of the music halls. She thought of nothing but clothes and parties and her dream of becoming a great star.

My old nerves reacted quite differently. I was very tired from all I had gone through and in a constant state of anxiety about the decision of the Comité d'Epuration. My job used up every bit of strength I could muster. I had to be free to put my whole mind on it. I still loved Nita and I think that if she hadn't changed we could have gone on together. But our lives were no longer in harmony. And so I had to make the terrible choice between her and my profession. As it always has, through my whole life, my job won out and, sadly, we parted to go our separate ways.

In the meantime I had my job to do—the job I have always loved beyond anything all my life.

I went back to work harder than ever. I was very busy developing a new routine, my one-man recitals. This absorbed every moment.

And so at the age of fifty-seven I set out on a whole new career which was to take me alone to all the cities of France and even back to Broadway and clear across the United States and Canada.

I have never been happier than I am now, free to do my own little specialty and to do it where I want.

I love my public. I love my job. It is my true *raison d'etre*. My life is very full. There are just three things that I no longer do. I do not smoke. I do not drink. And I do not—ski.